Selva armonica
(Rome, 1617)

Recent Researches in Music

A-R Editions publishes seven series of critical editions, spanning the history of Western music, American music, and oral traditions.

Recent Researches in the Music of the Middle Ages and Early Renaissance
    Charles M. Atkinson, general editor

Recent Researches in the Music of the Renaissance
    James Haar, general editor

Recent Researches in the Music of the Baroque Era
    Christoph Wolff, general editor

Recent Researches in the Music of the Classical Era
    Neal Zaslaw, general editor

Recent Researches in the Music of the Nineteenth and Early Twentieth Centuries
    Rufus Hallmark, general editor

Recent Researches in American Music
    John M. Graziano, general editor

Recent Researches in the Oral Traditions of Music
    Philip V. Bohlman, general editor

Each edition in *Recent Researches* is devoted to works by a single composer or to a single genre. The content is chosen for its high quality and historical importance and is edited according to the scholarly standards that govern the making of all reliable editions.

For information on establishing a standing order to any of our series, or for editorial guidelines on submitting proposals, please contact:

A-R Editions, Inc.
Middleton, Wisconsin 53562

800 736-0070 (North American book orders)
608 836-9000 (phone)
608 831-8200 (fax)
http://www.areditions.com

RECENT RESEARCHES IN THE MUSIC OF THE BAROQUE ERA, 141

Giovanni Francesco Anerio

Selva armonica (Rome, 1617)

Edited by Daniele V. Filippi

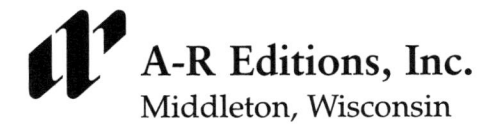

A-R Editions, Inc.
Middleton, Wisconsin

A Francesca

A-R Editions, Inc., Middleton, Wisconsin 53562
© 2006 by A-R Editions, Inc.

All rights reserved. No part of this book may be reproduced
or transmitted in any form by any electronic or mechanical
means (including photocopying, recording, or information
storage and retrieval) without permission in writing from
the publisher.

The purchase of this edition does not convey the right to
perform it in public, nor to make a recording of it for any
purpose. Such permission must be obtained in advance
from the publisher.

A-R Editions is pleased to support scholars and performers
in their use of *Recent Researches* material for study or performance. Subscribers to any of the *Recent Researches* series,
as well as patrons of subscribing institutions, are invited to
apply for information about our "Copyright Sharing Policy."

Printed in the United States of America

ISBN-13: 978-0-89579-588-5
ISBN-10: 0-89579-588-4
ISSN: 0484-0828

∞ The paper used in this publication meets the minimum
requirements of the American National Standard for
Information Sciences—Permanence of Paper for Printed
Library Materials, ANSI Z39.48-1992.

Contents

Acknowledgments   vii

Introduction   ix
  Devotional Music in Rome   ix
  The Composer   x
  The *Selva armonica*   xi
  Notes on Performance   xvi
  Notes   xvii

Texts and Translations   xxi

Plates   xxxvi

Selva armonica

  Dedication   2
    1. Sommo Re delle stelle   3
    2. Dal tuo volto beato   6
    3. Il tempo passa e mai più si ritrova   10
    4. O dolce amor, Gesù   14
    5. Acerbe doglie e voi, piaghe amorose   18
    6. Donna celeste, che di Dio sei Madre   20
    7. La matutina aurora   25
    8. Ecco riede, ecco soggiorna   28
    9. Pulchra es   29
  10. Veni sponsa Christi   34
  11. Regina caeli   36
  12. Ego flos campi   38
  13. Salve, Regina   41
  14. Salve Regina, Madre divina   45
  15. Gesù, nel tuo partire   49
  16. Ecco che i monti indora   54
  17. Alta cosa è il mio Dio   59
  18. Ecco vien fuor la notte   65
  19. Occhi del cielo ardenti   69
  20. Alzate al sommo ciel memoria e mente   76
  21. Torna la sera bruna   85
  22. Dio ti salvi, Maria, Madre divina   91
  23. O tu, che vai per via   97
  24. O del gran Redentor Madre alma e bella   103
  25. Ave Maria, Speranza mia   110
  26. Io non saprei dir quanto   114
  27. Litaniae Beatae Mariae Virginis   134

Critical Report   155
　Sources   155
　Editorial Methods   155
　Critical Notes   156
　Notes   158

Acknowledgments

It is a pleasant duty to acknowledge, first of all, the support I received from librarians working in the following institutions: the Biblioteca Nazionale Braidense, the Biblioteca del Conservatorio "Giuseppe Verdi," and the Biblioteca del Convento dei Cappuccini in Milan; the Biblioteca del Seminario Diocesano in Venegono Inferiore (Varese); the Biblioteca del Civico Museo Bibliografico Musicale in Bologna; and the Biblioteca Vallicelliana, the Biblioteca Nazionale Centrale Vittorio Emanuele II, the Biblioteca del Conservatorio di Santa Cecilia, and the Archivio Storico Capitolino in Rome. The staffs of the Ufficio Bibliografico and the University of Pavia's Biblioteca del Dipartimento di Scienze musicologiche e Paleografico-filologiche in Cremona have been especially helpful, in particular Dr. Renato Borghi. Research expenses for this project have been covered by the aforementioned musicology department in the University of Pavia.

I am grateful to Father Edoardo Cerrato, procurator general of the Confederation of the Oratory, for his enthusiastic encouragement, and to Father Alberto Venturoli, who escorted me in the Archive of the Congregation at the Chiesa Nuova in Rome. I would also like to express my gratitude to the scholars who gave me the benefit of their criticisms and suggestions: Rodobaldo Tibaldi and Antonio Delfino (who were my dissertation advisors during my years in Cremona), Maria Caraci Vela, Noel O'Regan, Giancarlo Rostirolla, Robert Kendrick, Lorenzo Bianconi, Arnaldo Morelli, Jonathan Couchman, Marco Della Sciucca, Vincenzo Borghetti, and Antonella D'Ovidio. I owe a great debt in particular to Claudio Vela, who patiently listened to and answered my questions about Italian poetry, and to Joachim Steinheuer, who played an important role in the very first conception of this project. Finally, I am most grateful to my dear colleague Lisa Navach, who, besides helping me with the translations (whose remaining imperfections are my sole responsibility), made many valuable observations, as usual.

Introduction

Giovanni Francesco Anerio's *Selva armonica* (1617)[1] is a miscellaneous, primarily devotional collection containing twenty-one Italian and six Latin compositions for one to four voices and basso continuo. The exploration of its textual and musical content allows a deeper understanding of spiritual music in post-Tridentine Italy. Its remarkable overlap of genres shows some of the manifold musical possibilities associated with contemporary devotional practices. Today Anerio is justifiably celebrated for his compositional skill, but he also deserves special attention because of his close connection with Filippo Neri (1515–95) and his Oratorio. A telling confirmation of this relationship is the fact that ten texts in the *Selva armonica* are taken from Agostino Manni's *Essercitii spirituali*, the most influential spirituality book of the early Oratorian tradition. This edition presents Anerio's collection for the first time in a modern critical edition and examines its contents within the context of the Roman Oratorio.

Devotional Music in Rome

The connection between art, prayer, and meditation played a central role in the cultural life of the late Italian cinquecento.[2] The art of music in particular had a special place in religious life, due in part to its effectiveness in suggesting certain structural elements of worship (inner harmony, elevation, repetition, intensification in the perception of sacred space, contact with the ineffable, etc.) and capturing intellect, senses, and bodily activity. Indeed, these characteristics make music the ideal support for prayer and, together with its *diletto* and its mnemonic properties, account for the frequent recourse to singing in post-Tridentine Christian life (singing took place during catechesis, paraliturgical meetings, pilgrimages and processions, and a number of other spiritual practices).

The invention (or reinvention) of spiritual musical genres—including the lauda (radiating from Rome in its Oratorian and Jesuitic palingenesis), spiritual madrigal, dialogue, canzonetta, and the various devotional reworkings of secular songs (with slightly recast texts)—also encouraged late cinquecento Catholics to embrace music as a means for devotion. Proliferation of these genres was favored by the spirit—if not by the letter—of the Council of Trent (1545–63), which catalyzed new artistic sensibilities and stimulated composers and poets to create devotional works infused with the principles of the conciliar reforms;[3] the new spiritual genres were modeled following basically the same guidelines given by conciliar decrees and other authoritative interventions for realizing sacred images.[4] These guidelines, as they applied specifically to music, called for clarity, simplicity, and intelligibility of both the language—achieved by use of vernacular texts—and the musical technique (the most learned spiritual madrigals constituted a partial exception from this point of view); they also included more general expectations that spiritual art reject any lascivious or immoral element, conform to church doctrine, educate its audience (as in vernacular translations of Latin prayers), and inspire devotion through sensations and emotions.

The production of devotional music involved some of the period's greatest composers (Palestrina, Monte, Marenzio, Lasso, to name but a few) and poets (e.g., Angelo Grillo, Torquato Tasso, Luigi Tansillo, and Giambattista Marino). The growing repertoire was enthusiastically supported by influential laymen and ecclesiastics, and assured by a many-sided world of performers and listeners (who resided in noble houses as well as in confraternities, academies, schools, and all sorts of religious institutions). Focusing on the Roman milieu, the main phenomenon in this context was no doubt the rebirth of the lauda. Filippo Neri and his Oratorians strongly encouraged the practice of singing these vernacular devotional songs, and their endorsement lead to an impressive succession of lauda publications, particularly from 1563 to the end of the century (edited at first by Giovanni Animuccia, then by Francisco Soto de Langa and Giovenale Ancina).[5] Roman composers also participated in other spiritual genres, although to a lesser degree; a small but significant number of spiritual canzonetta books were printed in the 1580s and 1590s (see especially the collections edited by Paolo Quagliati and Simone Verovio), and three Roman authors contributed to the spiritual madrigal repertoire (following the pioneering works by Cesare Tudino and Animuccia in 1564 and 1565, respectively),[6] with collections of settings for five voices: Palestrina (1581, published in Venice, and 1594), Marenzio (1584), and Felice Anerio (1585).[7]

The production of spiritual music in Rome continued into the seventeenth century, which opened with three highly significant Roman publications: the *Nuove laudi ariose della Beatissima Vergine* edited by Ancina and Giovanni Arascione (this collection concludes the laudistic series that began late in the previous century), the *Rappresentatione di Anima, et di Corpo* by Emilio de' Cavalieri, and the *Dialogo pastorale al presepio di nostro Signore* by Giovanni Francesco Anerio (all issued during the jubilee year 1600).[8] In 1608 Ottavio Durante included the first two spiritual madrigals with basso continuo ever published in Rome in his *Arie devote*. In the same period, other composers were still publishing whole collections of polyphonic spiritual madrigals (among them, the *Madrigali spirituali a quattro voci. Libro primo*, issued in 1608 by the minor figure Flaminio Oddi, is still extant today). Between 1616 and 1620, six important collections of concerted spiritual madrigals appeared in Rome, all issued by the printer Giovanni Battista Robletti: two books of *Scherzi sacri* by Antonio Cifra (1616 and 1618), the *Affetti amorosi spirituali* by Quagliati (1617),[9] and three works by Giovanni Francesco Anerio, namely the *Selva armonica* (1617), the *Teatro armonico spirituale* (1619), and the *Rime sacre* (1620).

Within this complex and varied corpus of Roman spiritual music (consisting of about thirty collections—some of which were reprinted—issued in six decades), some themes and typologies emerge in a remarkable way. The most prevalent topics include: prayers and invocations to the Lord; Marian devotion; Christmas; Christ's Passion and the Cross; repentance and the gift of tears; desire for conversion; mystical relationships with Christ; vanity of vanities; contempt for the world; and paraphrases of well-known prayers (e.g., "Ave Maria" and the hymn "Dulcis Jesu memoria"). Less frequent subjects are other episodes in the life of Jesus, invocation of the Holy Spirit, devotion to saints and angels, and the afterlife. Notably absent are such themes as the Eucharist, Easter, and theological-ecclesiological matters. In a general sense, one could say that despite the diverse derivation of these compositions, most give special emphasis to the sacred *affetti* and to moral aspects of religious life. Such themes are certainly appropriate for private devotional settings; perhaps more importantly, though, certain topics may have been preferred because of their particular suitability for expression in song (e.g., praise, spiritual *affetti*, and the like).

The Oratorians were among the most important patrons of spiritual poetry and music. In fact, their fundamental approach to any artistic expression was devotional; in other words, they intended artwork most of all as an instrument for prayer, a vehicle for spiritual elevation, or an allurement for novices.[10] The devotional aesthetic that clearly emerges in the writings of Ancina, among others, fits perfectly with Oratorian spirituality, espousing anti-intellectualism and lively communication.[11] Another prominent member of the Oratorio, Francesco Tarugi, synthesized its mission with these words: "Il compito del nostro istituto è di parlare al cuore" (the main task of our Congregation is speaking to men's hearts).[12]

The Composer

Giovanni Francesco Anerio (ca. 1569–1630) was born in Rome most likely in 1569 (and not in 1567 or 1570 as suggested in earlier musicological literature).[13] His father Maurizio Anerio (d. 1593), a native of Borgheria (near Narni), was a trombonist at S. Luigi dei Francesi from 1575 to 1582.[14] His mother Fulginia (d. 1599), also a native of Narni, was probably the composer Asprilio Pacelli's aunt. The couple's three sons, Felice (ca. 1560–1614), Giovanni Francesco, and Bernardino (d. 1595), all became musicians.[15] From the early 1550s, Fulginia had encouraged the whole family to become more involved with Filippo Neri (who was their confessor)[16] and his entourage, and from then on they were in close contact with the Oratorians. According to the *stato d'anime* of S. Cecilia a Monte Giordano parish, the Anerios lived at Pozzo Bianco, near the Vallicella, in the early 1580s.[17]

We do not know much about Giovanni Francesco's early education. Graham Dixon proposed to identify him with a "Giovanni Francesco" soprano at the Venerable English College in 1579.[18] We know that he took the minor orders in the 1580s,[19] and on 16 July 1598 was admitted "in choro" in the Oratorian community. On 16 November 1602 he was accepted into the Congregation (he had previously become a deacon), but for unknown reasons probably did *not* officially join.[20] He fulfilled his ecclesiastical career only in 1616, when he became a priest and celebrated his first mass at the Chiesa del Gesù, with splendid musical pomp, on 7 August 1616.[21] As correctly pointed out by Thomas F. Kennedy, although Anerio celebrated his first mass in the Jesuitic Mother Church and had been *prefetto della musica* at the Seminario Romano, he was *not* a Jesuit, but a diocesan priest.[22]

After his early training as a singer, Anerio's musical career began in the employment of Cardinal Antonio Maria Galli and Duke Massimiliano Caffarelli in the 1590s. He later became *maestro di cappella* at S. Giovanni in Laterano (between 1600 and 1605),[23] and at S. Spirito in Saxia (perhaps already in 1606, and certainly in 1608).[24] In November 1608 he was chosen as chapel master of the Duomo in Verona, where he began his service in the following summer (3 July 1609);[25] in 1610 he was also designated as *maestro di musica* of Verona's Accademia Filarmonica. In spite of the high wages and the brilliant musical life at these institutions, Anerio often visited Rome during his tenure and eventually left Verona for good in March 1611.[26] In July he began pursuing another appointment in northern Italy, at first in Milan; after the death of Giulio Cesare Gabussi, chapel master at the Duomo in Milan, Francisco Soto de Langa wrote to Cardinal Federico Borromeo (with whom the Oratorians had a close relationship), and in a commendatory letter recommended as the new chapel master

> a [former] pupil of ours at the Vallicella named signor Giovan Francesco Anerio, a forty-two-year-old man. As a young man he has been *maestro di cappella* at S. Giovanni in Laterano and other most noble churches, and he is at present *maestro di cappella* of the RR. Jesuits Fathers. . . . [Anerio would make a good chapel master] since he is gifted with the excellence in composing and conducting the chapel, as well as playing the organ, and he has studied also philosophy and other sciences.[27]

What is particularly striking in this letter is the professional profile it traces; besides Anerio's musical skills (his "excellence in composing and conducting the chapel, as well as playing the organ"), Soto de Langa emphasizes Anerio's extramusical education (studies in "philosophy and other sciences"). This special training may indeed have contributed to Anerio's refinement in text setting and his keen sensitivity to musical renditions of spiritual elements. The reference to the "RR. Jesuits Fathers" reminds us that in the meantime Anerio had become *praefectus musicae* at the Seminario Romano.[28] Unfortunately, Soto de Langa's proposal was not successful (nor was a reiterated recommendation issued by Duke Giovanni Angelo Altemps in September 1611),[29] but Anerio nonetheless continued to seek a prestigious position in northern Italy. In summer 1612 he applied as chapel master for Duke Francesco II Gonzaga—who had just succeeded his father in the duchy of Mantua—but, after the sudden death of Francesco II himself, the post, previously held by Claudio Monteverdi, was assigned to Sante Orlandi.[30] The Venetian reprint of Anerio's second book of motets (previously issued in Rome in 1611 and dedicated to Claudio Acquaviva, the superior general of the Jesuits) in this same year may have been an attempt at self-promotion for the Mantua position.

Anerio finally abandoned his plan to move north; in 1613 he became *maestro di cappella* at S. Maria dei Monti in Rome, a post he held until 1620. In 1621 he was still in Rome, but nothing is known about the years 1622–23. In June 1624 Anerio appeared as first organist in the feast of the novices at the conventual church of S. Teonisto in Treviso (in the presence of Bishop Vincenzo Giustiniani).[31] Anerio had arrived in Treviso probably by way of Venice, and it seems likely that his presence in the Veneto region was linked with preliminary arrangements for his appointment at the Polish court of Sigismund III; he succeeded Asprilio Pacelli there in 1624, shortly after his Treviso performance.[32] Anerio remained in Poland for the rest of his life, although he probably traveled occasionally to Italy.[33] In fact, he died in route between Poland and Italy, his death recorded on 12 June 1630 in Graz. It is difficult to determine whether he had intended to return for a short period (maybe in order to publish his Polish works) or for good. He may even have been undertaking a diplomatic/musical mission to the archducal court of Graz.[34]

Although his first printed work, *Il primo libro de madrigali a cinque voci*, dates from 1599, Anerio had been an esteemed composer of sacred music since at least the first half of the 1590s, as testified by the inclusion of thirty-five of his compositions for three to five voices in the manuscript Mus. 152 (1596) in the Biblioteca Nazionale Centrale Vittorio Emanuele II.[35] In the following decades, Anerio sent a large number of works to the press: in addition to the well-known *Dialogo pastorale* (1600) and the *Teatro armonico spirituale* (1619), he issued two books of polyphonic madrigals, six collections with basso continuo (four secular and two spiritual), a book of masses, at least seven collections of concertato motets, an extensive book of antiphons, two litany collections, one book of responsories for Christmas and one of vespers psalms, and a single instrumental publication, the *Gagliarde intavolate* (1607).[36] To this vast and variegated corpus one should obviously add the compositions in anthologies and manuscripts (which increase the number of his preserved masses to seventeen).[37]

The dedications in the prints attest to the relationships Anerio established with Roman ecclesiastics and noblemen of various prestiges. Particularly remarkable are his links with the Avila family (named in three dedications, including the *Selva armonica*) and with the Society of Jesus (dedications are devoted to eminent members Claudio Acquaviva, Ignigo de Guevara, and Muzio Vitelleschi). Pope Paul V himself figures among the dedicatees: Anerio composed the five-voice *Missa Paulina Burghesia* in his honor, a work preserved in manuscript at the Roman Biblioteca Casanatense and in the Santini Sammlung in Münster.[38]

Anerio emerges from this biographical sketch as a man with a solid education in both the humanities and ecclesiastical subjects, deeply affected by religious experience, and closely linked with the most dynamic organizations in the contemporary Roman Catholic Church (the Society of Jesus and the Filippine Oratorio). A musician whose career of forty years began in Rome (when Palestrina was still active) and ended in Poland (where he introduced the charismatic grandeur of the Roman polychoral style to King Sigismund's court), his role in the stylistic transformation of early seventeenth-century Roman music can no longer remain underestimated.

The *Selva armonica*

Selva armonica was printed in 1617 by Giovanni Battista Robletti (probably the most important music printer in Rome at the time)[39] with a dedication to the young Isabella Avila (born ca. 1607), a member of a Roman family of Spanish origin.[40] It appeared ten years after the earliest extant printed collection of Italian spiritual compositions with basso continuo (Severo Bonini's *Madrigali e canzonette spirituali* of 1607),[41] and was the third book of this kind to appear in Rome (together with Quagliati's *Affetti amorosi spirituali*).[42]

The Texts

SUBJECTS AND CONTEXT

The term *selva*, quite frequent in titles of musical and poetic collections of the late sixteenth and early seventeenth centuries, indicates the miscellaneous character of the book and the variety of its "musical flowers." Table 1 summarizes some stylistic features of the *Selva armonica* pieces. Within it there are twenty-one Italian and six Latin texts, the vast majority of which have sacred inspiration; only three Italian texts deal with profane, naturalistic subjects, and the last piece in the collection is encomiastic, praising the vocal qualities of the dedicatee. Two of the Latin texts are taken from the Song of Songs. The others set well-known prayers, such as the "Salve, Regina" and the litanies (it is worth noting that five out of six Latin texts are devoted to the Virgin Mary). Among the Italian pieces, five are related to preexistent texts: there are two different paraphrases of the "Ave Maria," a paraphrase of the "Salve, Regina," and another of "Alma Redemptoris Mater"; one text hints at a famous madrigal attributed to Alfonso d'Avalos. Three others recall the subject, structure, and imagery of the hymnody for lauds, vespers, and compline, respectively.

Besides devotion to the Virgin Mary (which inspires ten compositions), other subjects emerge, although with lesser prominence: Christ's Passion, death and the afterlife, and the emptiness of the world. Other texts invoke and praise the Lord or deal with the mystical relationship between Christ and the devout. At least six of these texts derive from the repertoire of the polyphonic lauda. Thanks to Giancarlo Rostirolla's research, we know of a few other instances in which madrigal-style compositions reuse laudistic texts, but the point of contact between the lauda and madrigal, up to now underestimated, deserves further investigation.[43] In the case of Anerio's *Selva armonica*, the presence of laudistic texts no doubt serves as another indicator linking the collection with the Oratorian tradition.

TABLE 1
Content Synopsis of Giovanni Francesco Anerio, *Selva armonica* (Rome, 1617)

Title	Scoring	Rubric	Author/text source	Subject/liturgical feast	Notes
1. Sommo Re delle stelle	*a 1*		Agostino Manni	praise of Christ's incarnation; Christmas	
2. Dal tuo volto beato	*a 1*		lauda repertoire	mystical love	
3. Il tempo passa e mai più si ritrova*	*a 1*	aria		vanity of vanities	
4. O dolce amor, Gesù	*a 1*		lauda repertoire	mystical love	
5. Acerbe doglie e voi, piaghe amorose	*a 1*		lauda repertoire	Passion	
6. Donna celeste, che di Dio sei Madre	*a 1*	canzonetta	lauda repertoire	BVM; Christmas	
7. La matutina aurora	*a 1*	canzonetta		nature	
8. Ecco riede, ecco soggiorna	*a 1*	aria		nature	
9. Pulchra es	*a 1*		Song of Sg. 4:7–10	BVM	Latin text
10. Veni sponsa Christi	*a 1*		antiphon from the Common of Virgins	feast of Virgins	Latin text
11. Regina caeli	*a 1*		Marian antiphon	BVM; Easter	Latin text
12. Ego flos campi	*a 1*		Song of Sg. 2:1–3	BVM	Latin text
13. Salve, Regina	*a 1*		Marian antiphon	BVM	Latin text
14. Salve Regina, Madre divina	*a 2*		Agostino Manni	BVM	based on Latin antiphon "Salve, Regina"
15. Gesù, nel tuo partire	*a 2*	dialogo	lauda repertoire	mystical love; Ascension	references the madrigal "Ancor che col partire"
16. Ecco che i monti indora	*a 2*		Agostino Manni	morning prayer	based on lauds hymnody
17. Alta cosa è il mio Dio	*a 2*		Agostino Manni	generic praise	
18. Ecco vien fuor la notte	*a 3*		Agostino Manni	night prayer	based on compline hymnody
19. Occhi del cielo ardenti	*a 3*			nature	
20. Alzate al sommo ciel memoria e mente	*a 3*		Agostino Manni	generic praise; Trinity	
21. Torna la sera bruna	*a 3*	aria	Agostino Manni	evening prayer	based on vespers hymnody

TABLE 1 continued

Title	Scoring	Rubric	Author/ text source	Subject/ liturgical feast	Notes
22. Dio ti salvi, Maria, Madre divina	a 4		Agostino Manni	BVM	based on Latin antiphon "Ave Maria"
23. O tu, che vai per via	a 4	dialogo		the soul facing death	
24. O del gran Redentor Madre alma e bella	a 4		Agostino Manni	BVM	based on Latin antiphon "Alma Redemptoris Mater"
25. Ave Maria, Speranza mia	a 4		Agostino Manni; lauda repertoire	BVM	based on Latin antiphon "Ave Maria"
26. Io non saprei dir quanto	a 4	canzone		encomium to dedicatee	
27. Litaniae Beatae Mariae Virginis	a 3		traditional prayer	BVM	Latin text

*Misattributed to Petrarch in *Nuovo Vogel*.

METRICAL FORMS

For an overview of the metrical forms set by Anerio, see table 2 and the comments to individual poems in the "Texts and Translations." The most peculiar feature of the collection from this point of view is the frequent recourse to free forms in rhymed couplets.[44] Strikingly absent, on the other hand, are sonnets,[45] tercets, and especially madrigals (in coeval spiritual collections such as those by Cifra and Quagliati, madrigals account for forty to sixty percent of the poems, and the same applies, for instance, to Giovanni Girolamo Kapsberger's *Libro secondo d'arie* of 1623). Remarkable too is the frequency of five-syllable lines (*quinari*). Other characteristics, however, such as the occasional presence of *ottava rima*, the predilection for quatrains, the marginality of parisyllabic lines, and the predominance of *versi piani* are fairly common in the Roman spiritual repertoire of these decades.

THE POET

Agostino Manni has been identified as the author of at least ten *Selva armonica* texts. Manni was born in 1547 in Cantiano, a little town in central Italy (near Gubbio), and died in Rome one year after the publication of the *Selva armonica* (on 25 November 1618).[46] After studying in Perugia he went to Rome where he met Filippo Neri, and he gradually became one of the most influential members of the *Congregazione dell'Oratorio*.[47] He is regarded as the most talented among the preachers and poets who flourished in the Congregation. Besides several ascetic, historical, and erudite works,[48] he wrote many laudas and in 1600 he provided Cavalieri with the libretto for his *Rappresentatione*.[49]

The poems that Anerio selected for *Selva armonica* had already appeared in one of Manni's prints. Manni presented them not simply as devotional poems, however, but as an integral part of his most successful work, the *Essercitii spirituali*.[50] This book in two parts rapidly became a highly esteemed self-training manual in prayer and spirituality, a best seller not only in Rome, but also in northern Italy.[51] A French translation also appeared in Paris (1613–15).

As to the original context of these poems, the cases of "Ave Maria, Speranza mia" (no. 25), "Sommo Re delle stelle" (no. 1), and "O del gran Redentor Madre alma e bella" (no. 24) are representative. The first appears in Manni's chapter on honoring the Virgin Mary, "Esercizi da farsi per onor della B. Vergine Maria Madre di Dio" (*esercizio primo*):

> It is essential to remember her [i.e., the Virgin Mary] in the heart and to represent her in the mind many times. Some guidelines for those who are not used to the *esercizi spirituali*: in the morning, he who wants to become one of her devotees should imagine her and picture her in the state in which the angel Gabriel found her, when the marvelous incarnation of the everlasting Word took place in her womb. Then he should greet her with great reverence, look at her with intent eyes and utter this salutation:
> SALUTATION
> *Ave Maria,*
> *Speranza mia* [the complete poem follows].[52]

The other two texts figure in the same chapter (*esercizio secondo*):

> The day after, [the devotee] should return to prayer; having collected his spirit, he should imagine to see the holy Mother with her blessed Son in her arms. Considering that he is the eternal Son, our highest and infinite good, in whom all the treasures of heaven are contained, he should venerate and love him with intimate affection, and desire to have him in the shrine of his own heart. Then he should kiss the ground, bowing his head and joining his hands, adoring him [i.e., Christ] and acknowledging him as his Lord and Savior of the world. During this adoration he should say the following laude:

TABLE 2
Metrical Synopsis of Italian Texts in Giovanni Francesco Anerio, *Selva armonica* (Rome, 1617)

Metrical type	Structure	Titles
ottava rima	octaves of hendecasyllables	Il tempo passa e mai più si ritrova (no. 3)
partial sonnet	quatrains of hendecasyllables	Acerbe doglie e voi, piaghe amorose (no. 5)
ode	hexastichic strophes of eleven and seven-syllable lines	Dal tuo volto beato (no. 2)
		O dolce amor, Gesù (no. 4)
		Io non saprei dir quanto (no. 26)
canzonetta	octaves of seven-syllable lines	Occhi del cielo ardenti (no. 19)
	quatrains of seven-syllable lines	La matutina aurora (no. 7)
		Ecco che i monti indora (no. 16)
		Ecco vien fuor la notte (no. 18)
		Torna la sera bruna (no. 21)
	pentastichic strophes of eleven-, seven-, and five-syllable lines	Donna celeste, che di Dio sei Madre (no. 6)
	heteromorphic strophes of eleven-, seven-, and five-syllable lines	Alzate al sommo ciel memoria e mente (no. 20)
	quatrains of eight-syllable lines	Ecco riede, ecco soggiorna (no. 8)
rhymed couplets	seven-syllable lines	*O tu, che vai per via (no. 23)
	five-syllable lines	Salve Regina, Madre divina (no. 14)
		Ave Maria, Speranza mia (no. 25)
	various line lengths	Sommo Re delle stelle (no. 1)
		†Gesù, nel tuo partire (no. 15)
		Alta cosa è il mio Dio (no. 17)
		†Dio ti salvi, Maria, Madre divina (no. 22)
		†O del gran Redentor Madre alma e bella (no. 24)

*Final quatrain rhymes *abab* ("dialogue + chorus" structure).
†Structure has haphazard irregularities.

LAUDE
Sommo Re delle stelle [the complete poem follows].
WARNING
After adoration and thanksgiving to Jesus Christ, [the devotee] should turn to the blessed Mother and pray to her with deep affection, that she intercede with her highest Son—whom she holds so happily in her arms and in her blissful heart—for the devotee, asking what favor she may want. And at the same time he should pray to her that she be so kind as to embrace all the sinners with the same tender and sweet affection with which she holds her little Son in her arms.... After that he should greet her with reverence and praise her with these words:
LAUDE
O del gran Redentor Madre alma e bella [the complete poem follows].[53]

INTERPRETATIONS

The question arises, how should one go about interpreting the musical setting of texts originally embedded in a book of spiritual exercises? The lack of documentation prevents drawing unambiguous conclusions. A few elements, however, may help to understand the origin and function of these compositions: (1) as mentioned above, the Oratorians held poetry and music in high esteem, and as their aesthetic had a strong devotional orientation, they often used these arts as tools for evangelisation; (2) Manni himself had been the organizer and author of other musical/dramatic performances, and the metrical and syntactical disposition of his poetry made it naturally fitting for musical settings; (3) Manni and Anerio had known each other since at least 1602;[54] and (4) the poetic text used by Anerio follows the readings of Manni's book faithfully (when compared with other printed and manuscript sources).

With these facts in mind, we can thus suppose that the choice to set the poems was the fruit of an agreement between the two disciples of Filippo Neri. The dedicatee could also have played an important role in the creation of the collection; a semiprivate form of such spiritual exercises may have been "performed" in the house of Anerio's patrons in Rome (the Avilas' mansion, where the composer himself had been living in the period 1614–16, was at Monte Giordano, not far from the Chiesa Nuova). But without discarding this fascinating hypothesis, it must be recognised that Manni's *esercizi* were conceived rather for individuals than for a community—public devotions traditionally followed the quite different scheme of the *oratorio,* as shaped by Filippo Neri himself. On the other hand, the Roman devotees who constituted Anerio's ideal audience were surely acquainted with Manni's popular book, and during a performance they would not have failed to recognise the texts and associate them with their original context (filled with a lavish store of imagery, *affetti,* and so on). Any performance of the work would thus have been transformed into a sort of semiprivate *esercizio spirituale,* in a typical Filippine mixture of *docere, delectare,* and *movere.*

Considering both the *Selva armonica* and the subsequent experimental *Teatro armonico spirituale* (significantly foreshadowed here by the two unattributed but surely Oratorian dialogues), we can acknowledge Anerio's creative way of combining poetry, music, and the divine rhetoric of prayer as his main contribution to the musical culture and the spirituality of his own time.

The Music

Selva armonica's twenty-seven compositions are largely ordered by voicing; only the last piece (the BVM litanies set for three voices) departs from the pattern (see table 3).[55] Within this order, a refined *varietas* (in subject matter as well as in linguistic, metrical, and tonal factors) regulates the succession of the compositions. There is also great variety in dimensions and macroformal aspects. Sixteen pieces (including the five single-voice Latin works) have a single *pars,* while the remaining eleven articulate into multiple *partes* (from two to six), generally following the strophic division of the text. The shortest composition is "Ecco riede, ecco soggiorna" (no. 8), at nineteen measures. It is also the only piece in which the music of the first strophe repeats exactly for the following verses. The "Litaniae Beatae Mariae Virginis" (no. 27, with 324 mm.), and "Io non saprei dir quanto" (no. 26, with 299 mm.), are on the opposite side of the dimensional spectrum, far surpassing the other pieces in length. The average length spans between the sixty-two measures of "Ecco vien fuor la notte" (no. 18) and the 181 of "Alzate al sommo ciel memoria e mente" (no. 20).[56]

Three compositions bear the indication "aria." This genre label does not convey textual characteristics; the texts of these pieces in fact differ significantly from a metrical point of view, unfolding in *ottava rima,* quatrains of octosyllables, and quatrains of heptasyllables, respectively. Instead, the characterization refers to the formal outline of the musical setting, i.e., a strophic structure manifesting over a bass line that repeats with only minor changes.

Two consecutive pieces are labeled "canzonetta." The late Renaissance canzonetta featured a polystrophic poem with an average of three to four strophes of three or four lines each. The strophes had a prevalence of hendecasyllables, with occasional insertion of seven- and five-syllable lines.[57] The musical setting was usually

TABLE 3
Organization of Giovanni Francesco Anerio, *Selva armonica* (Rome, 1617)

Title	Scoring	Parts	Measures Total/(internal parts)
1. Sommo Re delle stelle	C/T	1	93
2. Dal tuo volto beato	C/T	4	112 (29 + 28 + 31 + 24)
3. Il tempo passa e mai più si ritrova	C/T	3	122 (40 + 41 + 41)
4. O dolce amor, Gesù	C/T	3	106 (30 + 32 + 44)
5. Acerbe doglie e voi, piaghe amorose	C/T	2	71 (36 + 35)
6. Donna celeste, che di Dio sei Madre	C/T	4	151 (30 + 39 + 32 + 50)
7. La matutina aurora	C/T	4	92 (17 + 21 + 30 + 24)
8. Ecco riede, ecco soggiorna	C/T	1	19
9. Pulchra es	C/T	1	145
10. Veni sponsa Christi	C/T	1	66
11. Regina caeli	C/T	1	76
12. Ego flos campi	C/T	1	80
13. Salve, Regina	C/T	1	113
14. Salve Regina, Madre divina	C, B si placet	1	84
15. Gesù, nel tuo partire	C1, C2/T	1	110

TABLE 3 continued

Title	Scoring	Parts	Measures Total/(internal parts)
16. Ecco che i monti indora	C1, C2	4	124 (36 + 26 + 31 + 31)
17. Alta cosa è il mio Dio	C, T	1	122
18. Ecco vien fuor la notte	C1, C2, T	1	62
19. Occhi del cielo ardenti	C1, C2, Bar	3	103 (30 + 33 + 40)
20. Alzate al sommo ciel memoria e mente	C1, C2, B	6	181 (27 + 16 + 24 + 20 + 30 + 64)
21. Torna la sera bruna	C1, C2, B/Bar	5	117 (23 + 23 + 23 + 23 + 25)
22. Dio ti salvi, Maria, Madre divina	C1, C2, A, Bar	1	107
23. O tu, che vai per via	C, A, T, B	1*	135 (105 + 30)
24. O del gran Redentor Madre alma e bella	C, A, T, B	1	113
25. Ave Maria, Speranza mia	C1, C2, A, Bar	1	67
26. Io non saprei dir quanto	C, A, T, B	6	299 (33 + 47 + 58 + 54 + 60 + 47)
27. Litaniae Beatae Mariae Virginis	C1, C2, Bar	1†	324 (278 + 46)

*Internal measure count refers to the chorus at the end of the dialogue.
†Internal measure count refers to the concluding *Agnus Dei*.

characterized by the form AABB. The two *Selva armonica* canzonettas are substantially consistent with the typical features of the genre (in spite of the sharp distinction between their subjects), except that, unlike most polyphonic canzonetta settings, each strophe has different music.

The indication "dialogo" refers, as is evident, not to metrical or strictly formal matters, but to the dramaturgy of the text. While the term does not specify a precise musical form, the dramatic textual elements may obviously have a great deal of influence on how the music unfolds. Other definitions of genre appear only in the title page: "motetti" and "madrigali." While the former term relates to five of the six Latin pieces (the last, no. 27, belongs to the distinct genre of the litanies), it is probable that Anerio and Robletti used the latter as a comprehensive definition for all the Italian compositions that did not fit any of the aforementioned categories.

Generally speaking, the music in *Selva armonica* is carefully balanced, with extensive and ingenious use of melodic and harmonic formulas. Anerio's smooth, euphonic writing is largely free from pathetic excess. In effect, the music adheres to the Oratorian motto, "muovere e non far maravigliare" (to move [the audience], and not to stir wonder).[58] The compositional restraint must be regarded as a conscious aesthetic choice and not a product of naïveté, since Anerio was surely acquainted with avant-garde monodic styles and was an absolute master at contrapuntal construction. His refined style expresses intense *affetti* without indulging in sensual delight, following the guidelines included in many Oratorian writings of the period.

Anerio's music synthesizes various trends in late sixteenth- and early seventeenth-century Roman musical culture. His particular achievement is a monodic-concertato style that blends the rhythmic energy and colors of lighter genres (the lauda and canzonetta), the rich harmony and melodic elegance of the late Roman madrigal, and the contrapuntal technique of post-Palestrinian sacred music. This successful amalgam earned him the grand reputation of "musicorum aetate nostra nulli secundus" (second to no other musician in our age) among his contemporaries.[59]

Notes on Performance

Since the fairly common indication, "tutte queste si possono cantare in Soprano ed in Tenore" (all these compositions may be sung either by a soprano or by a tenor) appears in the source with regard to all the solo compositions (see the *Tavola* reproduced in pl. 4), performers may take this possibility into consideration.[60] The source also gives optional voicings for two pieces: a tenor may replace the canto secondo in the dialogue "Gesù, nel tuo partire," (no. 15), and the basso of "Salve Regina, Madre divina" (no. 14) may be performed with the canto as notated or omitted *si placet*. See the critical notes for the exact wording of the source rubrics.

Concerning the problem of ornamentation in this repertoire, a passage from Quagliati's dedication to Anna Maria Cesi in his *Affetti amorosi spirituali* seems particularly interesting: "gli stessi componimenti accarezzati prima, e favoriti da lei, quando tal volta s'è compiaciuta cantarli ed *abbellirli con le sue artificiose maniere* e soavissima voce . . ." (the same compositions [were] first cherished and favored by you, when you sometimes took pleasure in singing and *embellishing them with your artful manners* and most exquisite voice).[61] Notwithstanding the stylistic differences between Quagliati and Anerio, it seems clear from this kind of evidence—as well as from passages by Ancina, among others[62]—that, like most secular music of the time, the spiritual repertoire was performed with improvised ornamentation in those years. Performers are thus encouraged to apply judicious ornamentation (especially in cadential areas), in coherence with the sober stylistic attitude of Anerio's music.[63]

Continuo players may realize the basso continuo on the organ, harpsichord, or any suitable combination of instruments that is informed by historical performance practice. The music itself may provide clues to appropriate realizations, and performers should give special consideration to at least two elements: (1) Anerio's instrumental lines are basically *bassi seguenti*, and as such should not be harmonized too fully; and (2) the occasional imitation between the bass and the vocal line suggests the opportunity of creating imitative insertions in the realization as well, where convenient.[64]

Notes

1. See Daniele V. Filippi, "*Selva armonica*: Giovanni Francesco Anerio e la musica spirituale a Roma nel primo Seicento," 2 vols. (Ph.D. diss., Università degli studi di Pavia–sede di Cremona, 2004) for a detailed examination of Anerio's *Selva armonica*.

2. See Marc Fumaroli, *L'école du silence: Le sentiment des images au XVIIe siècle* (Paris: Flammarion, 1994).

3. This orientation may be seen clearly in prefaces and dedications; to choose one example: "Questi Salmi come tutte le altre mie compositioni date alla stampa, allora io reputo che abbiano conseguito il fin loro, quando sono cantate, ed udite da persone che, dal gusto di questo strepitoso rimbombo d'aria fra vilissimi corpi ristretta e percossa, ergono il desiderio agli eterni e perfettissimi concerti de' cori angelici nel Paradiso" (I consider that these *Salmi*—like all the compositions I sent to the press—reach their aim when they are sung and listened to by people, who, relishing this loud sound of air compressed and put into vibration among most humble bodies, elevate their desire to the eternal and most perfect concerts of the angelic choirs in heaven). See Costanzo Antegnati, *Salmi a otto voci* (1592), quoted in Gino Stefani, *Musica barocca 2: Angeli e sirene* (Milan: Bompiani, 1988), 128.

4. See, for instance, Daniele Menozzi, *Les images: L'église et les arts visuels* (Paris: Éditions du Cerf, 1991) and Costanza Barbieri, "*Invisibilia per visibilia*: S. Filippo Neri, le immagini e la contemplazione," in *La regola e la fama: San Filippo Neri e l'arte*, Museo del Palazzo di Venezia (Rome), 64–79 (Milan: Electa, 1995). In the slightly later *Contrasto musico* (1630), Grazioso Uberti importantly confirms that the two problems were commonly viewed as linked; in the fifth part of the dialogue, the theme of images follows almost automatically the discussion about the use of music in the church. See Grazioso Uberti, *Contrasto musico: Opera dilettevole*, facsimile ed. Giancarlo Rostirolla (Lucca: Libreria musicale italiana, 1991), 90.

5. On the lauda, see especially Giancarlo Rostirolla, Danilo Zardin, and Oscar Mischiati, *La lauda spirituale tra Cinque e Seicento: Poesie e canti devozionali nell'Italia della Controriforma—Volume offerto a Giancarlo Rostirolla nel suo sessantesimo compleanno*, ed. Giuseppe Filippi et al. (Rome: Istituto di bibliografia musicale, 2001).

6. *Bibliografia della musica italiana vocale profana pubblicata dal 1500 al 1700*, ed. Emil Vogel, Alfred Einstein, François Lesure, and Claudio Sartori, 3 vols., new ed. (Pomezia: Staderini, Minkoff, 1977) (= *Nuovo Vogel*; henceforth *NV*), 2767 and 85, respectively.

7. *NV* 2101 and 2103 (Palestrina), 1676 (Marenzio), and 66 (Anerio).

8. The *Dialogo pastorale* was until now Anerio's only complete work available in modern edition; see Giovanni Francesco Anerio, *Dialogo pastorale al presepio di nostro Signore*, ed. Arnaldo Morelli (Rome: Pro musica studium, 1983).

9. On Cifra and Quagliati, see Margaret Ann Rorke, "The Spiritual Madrigals of Paolo Quagliati and Antonio Cifra" (Ph.D. diss., University of Michigan, 1980).

10. See Barbieri, "*Invisibilia per visibilia*," 71 and 77. See also Alessandro Zuccari, "La politica culturale dell'Oratorio romano nella seconda metà del Cinquecento," *Storia dell'arte* 41 (1981): 77–112.

11. See Ancina's manuscript works in the Biblioteca Vallicelliana and especially his dedications and introductions to the *Tempio armonico*, a diplomatic edition of which is given in *Bibliografia delle opere dei musicisti bresciani pubblicate a stampa nei secoli 16. e 17.: Opere in antologie*, ed. Ruggero Del Silenzio (Florence: Leo S. Olschki, 2002). On Ancina and his *Tempio armonico*, see Elisabetta Crema, "Il *Tempio armonico* di Giovenale Ancina: Edizione e commento" (Ph.D. diss., Università degli Studi di Milano, 2005), first complete modern edition of the collection, and the report of the recent Ancina conference held in Saluzzo, 8–10 October 2004 (*Il tempio armonico: Giovanni Giovenale Ancina e le musiche devozionali nel contesto internazionale del suo tempo* (Lucca: Libreria musicale italiana, forthcoming).

12. Quoted in Edoardo Aldo Cerrato, *S. Filippo Neri: La sua opera e la sua eredità* (Pavia: n.p., 2002), 64. On this matter, see Daniele V. Filippi, "Spiritualità, poesia, musica: Per ricomprendere le esperienze oratoriane del Cinque-Seicento," *Annales Oratorii* 3 (2004): 91–137.

13. A variety of documentary evidence supports this point. First, in her deposition made at Filippo Neri's beatification inquiries (20 November 1595), Anerio's mother mentions Giovanni Francesco's miraculous recovery from fever in 1585, implemented by Filippo Neri's divine connections, "era di età di sedici anni" (when he was sixteen years old); see Giovanni Incisa della Rocchetta, Nello Vian, and Carlo Gasbarri, eds., *Il primo processo per San Filippo Neri: Nel codice vaticano latino 3798 e in altri esemplari dell'archivio dell'Oratorio di Roma*, 4 vols. (Vatican City: Biblioteca Apostolica Vaticana, 1957–63), 1:320. Second, the rubric "aetatis annorum vigintisex in circa" (about twenty-six years old) prefaces Anerio's own deposition in the beatification process (26 October 1595); ibid., 338. Third, Anerio himself confirms in the aforementioned deposition that the year of his

miraculous recovery was 1585, "l'anno che morse Gregorio Decimotertio, se ben mi ricordo" (in the year that pope Gregory XIII died, if I can remember); ibid. Fourth, a letter by Francisco Soto de Langa to Cardinal Federico Borromeo, dated 30 July 1611, describes Anerio as "homo di età di quarantadue anni" (a forty-two-year-old man). On this important letter, edited in Antonio Cistellini, *San Filippo Neri: L'Oratorio e la Congregazione oratoriana*, 3 vols. (Brescia: Morcelliana, 1989), 3:1970, see n27 below. The following dictionary entries provide biographical information on Anerio: *The New Grove Dictionary of Music and Musicians*, 2nd ed., s.v. "Anerio, Giovanni Francesco," by Klaus Fischer; *Die Musik in Geschichte und Gegenwart*, 2nd. ed., *Personenteil*, s.v. "Anerio, Giovanni Francesco," by Klaus Fischer; and *Dizionario Enciclopedico Universale della Musica e dei Musicisti*, *Le biografie*, s.v. "Anerio, famiglia," by Sergio Durante. For other biographical sketches, see especially Wayne C. Hobbs, "Giovanni Francesco Anerio's *Teatro armonico spirituale di madrigali*: A Contribution to the Early History of the Oratorio" (Ph.D. diss., Tulane University, 1971), 110ff., and Nyal Z. Williams, "The Masses of Giovanni Francesco Anerio: A Historical and Analytical Study with a Supplementary Critical Edition" (Ph.D. diss., The University of North Carolina–Chapel Hill, 1971), 1–7.

14. See Alberto Cametti, "Nuovi contributi alle biografie di Maurizio e Felice Anerio," *Rivista musicale italiana* 22 (1915): 122–32 (esp. 127). Maurizio's brother Giovanni Battista was a priest and made a deposition at Filippo Neri's beatification inquiries (see Incisa della Rocchetta, Vian, and Gasbarri, *Primo processo*, 1:410–12).

15. Cametti, "Nuovi contributi," 130, mentions a daughter who became a nun before 1579. Bernardino was a cornettist at S. Luigi dei Francesi (from 1577 on), and later a singer for the Confraternita del SS. Crocifisso at S. Marcello (see, for example, Williams, "Masses of Giovanni Francesco Anerio," 1). As to Felice's biography, see especially Jonathan P. Couchman, "Felice Anerio's Music for the Church and for the Altemps Cappella" (Ph.D. diss., University of California–Los Angeles, 1989), which includes useful elements about Giovanni Francesco as well. Other members of the family, such as Massimo (Fulginia's brother-in-law), were also musicians.

16. As stated by Fulginia and Giovanni Francesco at the beatification inquiries. Fulginia had been Filippo Neri's personal laundress for thirty years (see Incisa della Rocchetta, Vian, and Gasbarri, *Primo processo*, 1:320).

17. See Cametti, "Nuovi contributi," 129. Arnaldo Morelli, *Il tempio armonico: Musica nell'Oratorio dei Filippini in Roma (1575–1705)*, Analecta musicologica, vol. 27 (Laaber: Laaber-Verlag, 1991), 16, n52, states that "almeno dal 1590 gli Anerio furono affittuari di una casa nei pressi della Chiesa Nuova, di proprietà della Congregazione. Dal 1597 a pagare l'affitto provvede personalmente Felice fino al settembre 1605, mese in cui è registrato l'ultimo pagamento degli Anerio" (at least from 1590 on, the Anerios rented a house near the Chiesa Nuova owned by the Congregation. From 1597 until September 1605, the date of the last recorded payment by the Anerios, it was Felice who personally saw to the payments). See also Couchman, "Felice Anerio's Music," 63.

18. Graham Dixon, "Music in the Venerable English College in the Early Baroque," in *La musica a Roma attraverso le fonti d'archivio*, ed. Bianca Maria Antolini, Arnaldo Morelli, and Vera Vita Spagnuolo, 470 (Lucca: Libreria musicale italiana, 1994).

19. He received the tonsure on 17 December 1583, the ostiariate on 22 December 1584, and the lectorate on 20 December 1586 (see Incisa della Rocchetta, Vian, and Gasbarri, *Primo processo*, 1:338, n870).

20. See Rostirolla, Zardin, and Mischiati, *Lauda spirituale*, 54–56 and Morelli, *Tempio armonico*, 16–17.

21. See the well-known description of the ceremony in Giacinto Gigli, *Diario romano (1608–1670)*, ed. Giuseppe Ricciotti (Rome: Tumminelli, 1958), 37.

22. See Thomas F. Kennedy, "Jesuits and Music: The European Tradition 1547–1622" (Ph.D. diss., University of California–Santa Barbara, 1982), 185.

23. See the different opinions expressed by Morelli (in the introduction to his edition of Anerio's *Dialogo pastorale*), by Wolfgang Witzenmann ("Materiali archivistici per la Cappella lateranense nell'Archivio capitolare di San Giovanni in Laterano," in *Musica a Roma*, 459 and 466), and in the various biographical dictionary entries (see n13 for citation of specific dictionaries). Because payrolls are lacking for some years, it is quite hard to determine precisely the periods of service.

24. See Antonio Allegra, "La cappella musicale di S. Spirito in Saxia di Roma," *Note d'archivio per la storia musicale* 17 (1940): 26–38 (esp. 30). Allegra clarifies the importance of this institution, strictly linked with the Papacy, and its musical chapel. Concerning the dates of Anerio's association with S. Spirito, it is worth noting that a recently published catalogue lists a "Salve, Regina" by him, included in a manuscript from S. Spirito dated 1603. See Dieter Haberl, ed., *Bischöfliche Zentralbibliothek Regensburg: Thematischer Katalog der Musikhandschriften* (München: Bibliothek Franz Xaver Haberl, 2000), see index.

25. Bishop Alberto Valier possibly played an important role in Anerio's appointment: In 1606 Alberto had succeeded his uncle, Cardinal Agostino, who was an intimate friend of Filippo Neri and a frequent visitor of the Oratorio.

26. See Antonio Spagnolo, *Le scuole accolitali in Verona* (Verona: G. Franchini, 1905), 100–102 (although not entirely free from errors), and Enrico Paganuzzi et al., *La musica a Verona* (Verona: Banca mutua popolare, 1976), 197 and 199.

27. "Un allievo della nostra Vallicella, nominato il signor Giovan Francesco Anerio, homo di età di quarantadue anni, che di giovane è stato maestro di cappella di S. Giovanni Laterano e d'altre nobilissime chiese, et è al presente maestro di cappella delli RR. Padri Gesuiti.... Poiché le sue qualità non si estendono solamente nell'eccellenza del comporre et regger cappelle, ma anco in sonar l'organo, havendo anco studiato filosofia et altre scienze." The letter is quoted according to the version in Cistellini, *San Filippo Neri*. It has now been edited (without any comment about Anerio due to the "Milanese" perspective of the book) also in Robert L. Kendrick, *The Sounds of Milan, 1585–1650* (Oxford: Oxford University Press, 2002), 387–88.

28. He succeeded Annibale Orgas (see Kennedy, "Jesuits and Music," 184). Since some biographies mistakenly refer to the Collegio Romano, it is worth specifying that the *Seminario Romano* (instituted by Pope Pious IV in 1565), although entrusted to the Jesuits, was dedicated to the formation of diocesan priests, while the *Collegio Romano* was *ab origine* (1551) an institution pertaining to the Society of Jesus. See, for instance, Agostino Borromeo, "I vescovi italiani e l'applicazione del Concilio di Trento," in *I tempi del Concilio: Religione, cultura e società nell'Europa Tridentina*, ed. Cesare Mozzarelli and Danilo Zardin, 68–69 (Rome: Bulzoni, 1997), and the literature suggested there.

29. The duke, patron of Felice Anerio, was a cousin of Cardinal Borromeo. The letter, dated 7 September 1611 reads: "Intendendo che è vacato il loco di Maestro di Capella di cotesta sua Cattedrale, non posso far di meno di non raccomandare a V.S. Ill.ma la persona di Giovanni Francesco Anerio, attissima a detto carico, assicurandomi per l'esperienza che ho di lui, che V.S. Ill.ma n'habbi da ricevere ogni satisfattione, il che promettendomi del suo favore, et del credito che darà a questa mia, non li starò a narrare le qualità di detto Francesco, essendo noto, et a V.S. Ill.ma bacio le mani" (Having heard that the position of *Maestro di Capella* in your Cathedral is vacant, I cannot help but commend to Your Most Illustrious Lordship a man very apt to this charge, Giovanni Francesco Anerio. Given the knowledge I have of him, I am sure that Your Most Illustrious Lordship will be fully satisfied. Thus, since I feel sure that you will accord your favor and give credit to this recommendation, I do not need to enumerate the well-known gifts of the said Francesco, and I kiss the hands of Your Most Illustrious Lordship). See Couchman, "Felice Anerio's Music," 168.

30. See Antonio Bertolotti, *Musici alla corte dei Gonzaga in Mantova dal secolo XV al XVII* (Milan: Ricordi, 1890), 77.

31. See Giuseppe D. Liberali, "Giovanni Francesco Anerio: Un suo fugace soggiorno a Treviso e le esecuzioni corali-

strumentali al monastero di S. Teonisto dal 1559 al 1667," *Note d'archivio per la storia musicale* 17 (1940): 171–78.

32. See Hellmut Federhofer, "Nochmals zur Biographie von Giovanni Francesco Anerio," *Die Musikforschung* 6 (1953): 346–47. According to Aleksandra Patalas, "Polish-Italian Relations in Music During the First Half of the Seventeenth Century" (unpublished paper read at the Seventh Biennial Conference on Baroque Music, Birmingham, UK, 1996), the Jesuits may have been responsible for the recruitment of Italian musicians for Sigismund.

33. At least two editions of his music were issued in Rome in those years: the *Litaniae Deiparae Virginis* (1626, printed by Masotti) and the arranged reprint of the *Responsorii della Natività* (1629, printed by Robletti).

34. On the possibility of a diplomatic/musical mission, see Hellmut Federhofer, "Ein Beitrag zur Biographie von Giovanni Francesco Anerio," *Die Musikforschung* 2 (1949): 210–13. Zygmunt M. Szweykowski is inclined to believe, on the other hand, in a temporary return. See his "Le messe di Giovanni Francesco Anerio ed il loro rapporto con l'attività del compositore in Polonia," *Quadrivium* 16 (1975): 145–52.

35. See *Catalogo del fondo musicale della Biblioteca Nazionale Centrale Vittorio Emanuele II di Roma*, with a historical introduction by Arnaldo Morelli (Rome: Consorzio IRIS per la valorizzazione dei beni librari, 1989).

36. For a list of Anerio's printed works (and of his dedications), see Filippi, "Selva armonica," 1:136–37.

37. See Williams, "Masses of Giovanni Francesco Anerio," 36; he does not include the two Polish polychoral masses: *Missa Pulchra es* (based on the five-voice motet by Palestrina and preserved in mscr. Kk. I. 83 of the Archive of the Cathedral Chapter in Kraków) and *Missa Constantia* (in the Biblioteca del Civico Museo Bibliografico Musicale). Modern editions of these masses are available: Giovanni Francesco Anerio, *Missa Pulchra es: Per due cori*, ed. Aleksandra Patalas (Kraków: Musica iagellonica, 1995) and Giovanni Francesco Anerio, *Missa Constantia: Per tre cori*, ed. Zygmunt M. Szweykowski (Kraków: Musica iagellonica, 1997). The best catalogue of Anerio's works in anthologies and manuscripts and of modern editions is still Hobbs, "Giovanni Francesco Anerio's *Teatro armonico*," 129–35 (although it needs updating and revisions in many respects). Regarding the sacred works composed by Anerio for the Altemps chapel, see the register in Luciano Luciani, "Le composizioni di Ruggero Giovannelli contenute nei due codici manoscritti ex Biblioteca althaempsiana, detti *Collectio major* e *Collectio minor*," in *Ruggero Giovannelli "musico eccellentissimo e forse il primo del suo tempo*," ed. Carmela Bongiovanni and Giancarlo Rostirolla, 281–318 (Palestrina: Fondazione Giovanni Pierluigi da Palestrina, 1998).

38. See Williams, "Masses of Giovanni Francesco Anerio," 41 and 46. The indication "auctore Ioanne Francisco Anerio *sacerdote* romano" in the Casanatense manuscript could suggest that the mass follows Anerio's ordination (1616), but the dating of this manuscript and its relation with the date of composition have not been explored yet.

39. See Saverio Franchi, *Le impressioni sceniche: Dizionario biobibliografico degli editori e stampatori romani e laziali di testi drammatici e libretti per musica dal 1579 al 1800*, 2 vols. (Rome: Edizioni di storia e letteratura, 1994–2002), 1:644–50. Robletti (ca. 1583–1655) was active in Rome, Tivoli, and Rieti in the years 1609–51. He issued high-quality editions of works by Francesco Soriano, Giovanni Bernardino Nanino, Romano Micheli, Kapsberger, and his close friends Quagliati and Cifra.

40. Anerio was Isabella's music teacher, as is made clear in the dedication. Two years later, he dedicated another collection to her, the *Ghirlanda di sacre rose* (1619): "ho risoluto dedicarla a Lei come a mia, non dirò più scolara (essendo oramai arrivata a termine tale nella musica, in così tenera età di dodici anni in che si ritrova) che non se li conviene più simil nome, ma sibbene a mia signora e padrona" (I resolved to dedicate it [i.e., the *Ghirlanda*] to You, no longer as to a pupil of mine [since you attained such a high level in music, at the tender age of twelve], because this name is no longer appropriate for you, but to my lady and patroness). Isabella most probably was the daughter of Girolama Cecchini and Giacomo Avila; see Dirk van [Teodoro] Ameyden, *La storia delle famiglie romane*, ed. Carlo Augusto Bertini, 2 vols. (Rome: Collegio araldico, [1910–14]; repr. Bologna: Forni, 1967), 1:93–94. Among Isabella's brothers are Tiberio (dedicatee of Anerio's *I lieti scherzi* of 1621), who delivered an oration "De laudibus Sancti Philippi Nerii" at the Vallicella in 1610 (later published by Bartolomeo Zannetti), and Giuseppe Maria, ecclesiastic and writer, later bishop of Campagna, near Salerno. The family enjoyed the patronage of the powerful Aldobrandinis and was closely linked with the Filippine Oratorio (see Morelli, *Tempio armonico*, 17, n54, and Cistellini, *San Filippo Neri*, 3:1947). The Avilas' coat of arms is included on the title page of the *Selva armonica* (see pl. 1). For further details and literature on the family, see Filippi, "Selva armonica," 1:148–55.

41. *NV* 391. See Jerome Roche, "On the Border Between Motet and Spiritual Madrigal: Early 17th-Century Books that Mix Motets and Vernacular Settings," in *Seicento inesplorato: L'evento musicale tra prassi e stile—un modello di interdipendenza*, ed. Alberto Colzani, Andrea Luppi, and Maurizio Padoan, 310 (Como: AMIS, 1993).

42. The first and second were Durante's *Arie devote* (1608) and Cifra's first book of *Scherzi sacri* (1616). See *NV* 887 (Durante), 566 (Cifra), and 2290 (Quagliati).

43. See Rostirolla, Zardin, and Mischiati, *Lauda spirituale*, 208–9.

44. Rhymed couplets are to be found also in Quagliati's *Affetti amorosi spirituali*, but usually within strophic forms. As to the systematic adoption of rhymed couplets in both canzonetta structures and in larger poems by Gabriello Chiabrera, see Francesco Bausi and Mario Martelli, *La metrica italiana: Teoria e storia* (Florence: Le lettere, 1993), esp. 182.

45. Anerio set sonnets in his other collections, e.g., *Rime sacre*, but largely excluded them in the *Selva armonica*; the collection includes only the first half of the sonnet "Acerbe doglie e voi, piaghe amorose" (no. 5).

46. Manni's importance has been up to now underestimated both by musicologists and scholars of other disciplines; for the most part, information about his life has been scattered in historical literature concerning the Oratorians and minor publications—such as Domenico Luchetti, *Picccola biografia del p. Agostino Manni* (Gubbio: Soc. tipografica "Oderisi," 1938) and Agostino Manni, *Laudi, prieghi, hinni ecc.* [sic], ed. Domenico Luchetti (Gubbio: Soc. tipografica "Oderisi," 1947)—see Warren Kirkendale, *Emilio de' Cavalieri "gentiluomo romano": His Life and Letters, His Role as Superintendent of All the Arts at the Medici Court, and His Musical Compositions* (Florence: Leo S. Olschki, 2001), 245ff., and Guglielmo Guglielmi, *La vita e le opere del padre Agostino Manni dell'Oratorio di S. Filippo Neri: Nel 450° anno della sua nascita, 1547–1997* (Bologna: Bologna University Press, 1997); the latter consists mainly of a poetic anthology.

47. He entered the Congregation in 1577 and was ordained a priest on 19 March 1580. See *Dictionnaire de spiritualité ascétique et mystique: Doctrine et histoire*, s.v. "Manni, Augustin," by Carlo Gasbarri. In 1596, after the death of the founder, Manni obtained the prestigious office of *prefetto dell'Oratorio piccolo de' secolari* (see Cistellini, *San Filippo Neri*, 2:1047).

48. See the list in Kirkendale, *Emilio de' Cavalieri*; see also Suzanne P. Michel and Paul-Henri Michel, *Répertoire des ouvrages imprimés en langue italienne au XVIIe siècle conservés dans les bibliothèques de France*, 8 vols. (Paris: Éditions du Centre national de la recherche scientifique, 1967–84), 5:97, and Massimo Ceresa, *Una stamperia nella Roma del primo Seicento: Annali tipografici di Guglielmo Facciotti ed eredi (1592–1640)* (Rome: Bulzoni, 2000), see index.

49. See Kirkendale, *Emilio de' Cavalieri*. For a metrical analysis of the *Rappresentatione* see Filippi, "Selva armonica," 162–66.

50. According to Cistellini, a decree of the Congregation on 27 January 1606 authorized Manni to publish the *Essercitii* for the first time. Although no exemplar of the first edition is

extant, the book was most probably issued during the same year. Moreover, another decree of May 1607 allowed Manni to print an expanded edition that, according to the indication on the title page, was issued by Guglielmo Facciotti (Rome, 1607): "seconda impressione dall'istesso autore in molti luoghi accresciuta." See Cistellini, *San Filippo Neri*, 3:1767 and 1829. In 1613 Giacomo Mascardi published a "quarta impressione" at the request of Pietro Grialdi; the third Roman impression may be that of 1608, also issued by Mascardi, of which the second volume is preserved. The success of Manni's works lasted for various decades. See Michel and Michel, *Répertoire des ouvrages imprimés en langue italienne*, 5:97. A posthumous collection containing many of his spiritual poems and writings was edited by his friend and fellow citizen Francesco Maggioli, with the title *Valle di gigli e rose per ricreare l'anima che sta afflitta tra le spine del mondo* (Rome: Guglielmo Facciotti at the request of Pietro Grialdi, 1619).

51. The edition used for the present research was issued in Brescia by Bartolomeo Fontana in 1609 in two volumes: the first measures 70 x 100 mm, with xvi + 320 + xvi pages and a dedication by the printer dated 14 March 1609, the second 71 x 130 mm, with 608 + xvi pages and a dedication by the printer dated 28 May 1609. The complete titles of the two volumes read as follows:

Essercitii spirituali di Agostino Manno da Cantiano, Prete della Congregatione dell'Oratorio di Roma. Dove si mostra un modo facile per fare fruttuosamente oratione a Dio, et di pensare cose che principalmente appartengono alla salute, di acquistare il vero dolore de peccati e di fare una felice morte. Con tre essercitii per diventare devoto della Beatissima Vergine Maria Madre di Dio.

Essercitii formati dal P. Agostino Manno da Cantiano della Congregatione dell'Oratorio di Roma. Parte seconda. Dove si mostra come si possa con i pensieri ordinati far presto, & sicuro profitto nella scienza della salute, & inalzare l'animo alla consideratione della Grandezza di Dio, & all'affetto del sommo bene: et un'Ethica Christiana per conoscere lo splendore delle virtù, & infamia de' vitii, & costumi del Mondo: con un Compendio di ammaestramenti del Padre Filippo Neri: et un Ragionamento dell'onnipotenza dell'Oratione.

52. È necessario ogni giorno rammemorarla dentro al cuore e rappresentarla nella mente più volte. E per dare un poco d'ordine a quelli che non sono soliti a gli esercizi spirituali, potrà, chi desidera di esserli devoti [sic], la mattina informare l'immaginazione su di lei, e rappresentarsela in quel modo che fu trovata quando fu salutata dall'Angelo, all'ora che fu fatta nel suo ventre la maravigliosa Incarnazione del sempiterno Verbo, e formata l'immaginazione salutarla con profonda riverenza, ed affissatili gli occhi addosso, subito soggiongerli questa salutazione: | SALUTAZIONE | *Ave Maria,* | *speranza mia*. Manni, *Essercitii spirituali*, 1:61ff. Emphasis added.

53. All'altro giorno torni all'orazione e, raccolto lo spirito, facci un'immaginazione di veder questa santissima Madre col suo benedetto Figliuolo in braccio, e considerando che quello ch'essa abbraccia è l'eterno Figliuolo, sommo ed infinito bene nostro, nel quale si rinchiudono bene tutti i tesori del cielo, muova l'affetto suo a venerarlo ed amarlo, e desideri averlo nell'arca del suo cuore: ed inchinando la testa e giungendo le mani baci la terra e lo adori e riconosca per suo Signore e Salvator del Mondo, ed adorandolo dica questa laude: | LAUDE | *Sommo Re delle stelle....* | AVVISO | Fatta l'adorazione e 'l rendimento di grazie a Gesù Cristo, rivolgasi alla beata Madre e la preghi con ogni affetto che, poiché con tanta sua felicità tiene il sommo suo Figliuolo nell'amorose sue braccia e nel felice suo cuore, si degni porgergli un priego per lui, domandandogli quella grazia che a lei più piaccia; soggiungendoli insieme, che con quell'affetto tenero e dolce col quale Ella tiene abbracciato il Figliuolo suo, si degni abbracciare tutti i peccatori.... Fatto questo riverentemente la saluti e la laudi con queste parole: | LAUDE | *O del gran Redentor Madre alma e bella*. Manni, *Essercitii spirituali*, 1:75ff. Emphasis added.

54. See a document from the Archivio della Congregazione dell'Oratorio di Roma alla Chiesa Nuova, edited in Morelli, *Tempio armonico*, 114 (doc. 57). In November 1602 Manni was asked, together with another brother, to evaluate Anerio's eligibility before the admission in the Congregation.

55. On the frequency of this order in coeval Roman collections, see Paolo Fabbri, Angelo Pompilio, and Antonio Vassalli, "Frescobaldi e le raccolte con composizioni a voce sola del primo Seicento," in *Girolamo Frescobaldi nel IV centenario della nascita*, ed. Sergio Durante and Dinko Fabris, 241 (Florence: Leo S. Olschki, 1986).

56. "Pulchra es" (no. 9; 145 mm.) is the longest among the compositions in one part, except for the litanies (no. 27).

57. See Concetta Assenza, *La canzonetta dal 1570 al 1615* (Lucca: Libreria musicale italiana, 1997), 137.

58. See Arnaldo Morelli, "*Il muovere e non il far maravigliare*: Relationships between Artistic and Musical Patronage in the Roman Oratory," *Italian History and Culture* 5 (1999): 13–28.

59. From the preface to the second part of Anerio's *Antiphonae seu sacrae cantiones* (1613) by Roberto Belando. For a broad analytical approach to the *Selva armonica*, see Filippi, "*Selva armonica*," 1:159–349.

60. Other indications in the Basso dell'organo partbook confirm this opportunity (e.g., p. 16, "Canto solo ovvero tenore solo").

61. Cited and translated in Rorke, "Spiritual Madrigals," 44. Emphasis added.

62. See for instance his well-known dedication of the *Tempio armonico della Beatissima Vergine* (1599) to Geronima Colonna, where he mentions various virtuoso singers and players.

63. The apparent clash between some precadential figures in the continuo and the corresponding melodic lines can be emended only by an opportune agreement among the performers (on the basis of the musical text, but beyond it). It is frequent, for instance, to find a conflict between the figure 4 in the continuo and 3 sung in a vocal part (see e.g., "Io non saprei dir quanto" [no. 26], m. 64), or vice versa (see "Litaniae Beatae Mariae Virginis" [no. 27], m. 252). To judge from these kinds of passages, the value of the continuo figures themselves could be questioned (did someone add them on behalf of the composer at the last stage of the editorial production, without looking at the vocal parts?). Or, given the incompleteness of the figures, one could even suggest that continuo players were commonly supposed to use a keyboard tablature; realized continuo parts in manuscript belonging to the same repertoire (see for instance Anerio's "Ritorn'al tuo pastor, smarrit'agnella," part 1, m. 22, in Biblioteca Vallicelliana Ms. Z.122–30) show, however, similar clashes with the vocal parts. Unless we hypothesize that such conflicts were accepted in the performance practice, we should postulate the aforesaid *flexible agreement among the performers on the basis of the musical text*, particularly in the preparation and organization of cadential events.

64. See at least Helmut Haack, *Anfänge des Generalbaßsatzes: Die "Cento concerti ecclesiastici" (1602) von Lodovico Viadana*, 2 vols. (Tutzing: Hans Schneider, 1974), 1:207–8.

Texts and Translations

The translations reflect the original language as accurately as possible, but sometimes adjust the syntax in order to achieve sense in English. As regards the graphical criteria adopted in the edition, the following changes to the original forms have been made: Punctuation and graphic forms of the Latin texts follow the *Antiphonale Romanum* (in "Veni sponsa Christi" [no. 10], "Regina caeli" [no. 11], "Salve, Regina" [no. 13], and "Litaniae Beatae Mariae Virginis" [no. 27]) or the *Vulgata* (in "Pulchra es" [no. 9] and "Ego flos campi"[no. 12]). Italian punctuation and accents have been integrated and modernized, and the only instance of diaeresis has been marked (*oriënte*). The use of the apostrophe has been normalized in order to avoid ambiguity of pronunciation and meaning (e.g., *de'* becomes *de'* wherever appropriate; *e l'* and *el* both become *e 'l*; *ch'a d'una* becomes *ch'ad una*; *c'hai* becomes *ci hai* wherever appropriate; *gl'agricoltori* becomes *gli agricoltori*; *quegl'occhi* becomes *quegli occhi*; *ogn'augel* becomes *ogni augel*; *prend'il mio cor* becomes *prende il mio cor*; *ced'e* becomes *cede e*). Consistent forms such as *l'onde, l'altezze, all'ombre, ch'ha* (and similar cases) have been maintained.

Besides the standard capitalization of the first letter of each poetic line, capitalization conforms to modern usage. Internal words are set in lower case unless they are references to God or the Virgin Mary, *senhal* references to the dedicatee (e.g., *Cicala*; *Sirenetta*), or other proper nouns. The personification *Morte* is capitalized as well. The graphic forms *&* and *et* have been rendered as *e* before words beginning with a consonant or as *ed* before words beginning with a vowel. The use of *h* has been normalized and the etymological *h* eliminated (e.g., *hinno/hinni* becomes *inno/inni*; *Christo* becomes *Cristo*). The *i* devoid of diacritical function has also been omitted (e.g., *Giesù* becomes *Gesù*; *messaggiero* becomes *messaggero*). The spelling *ti* for the dental affricate has been replaced with *zi* (e.g., *gratia/gratie* becomes *grazia/grazie*). Double and single consonants have been normalized in accordance with modern usage (*fabro* and *sapiamo* become *fabbro* and *sappiamo*, but *maggione* and *ruggiada* become *magione* and *rugiada*). Forms such as *amira, avampi/avampano, commun, del'[aura], doppo, imago, matutina,* and *provisione* are preserved, however. The double form *core/cuore* is retained. Likewise, synthetic forms have been retained wherever possible (unless otherwise indicated in the critical notes) and always adopted for *ogn'or* (*ognor*), *pur che* (*purché*), and *sin che* (*sinché*). Analytic forms, however, such as *a i, a le, a l'un, da le, ne gli, de gli, già mai,* and *se ben* have been chosen when consistent.

Comments following the texts record structural and idiosyncratic features of the poetry, additional text sources and musical settings, and spelling and language variants in concordant sources (spelling discrepancies in the primary source are recorded in the critical report following the music). The following sigla and abbreviations are used in the comments: I-Rn = Biblioteca Nazionale Centrale Vittorio Emanuele II, Rome ; I-Rv = Biblioteca Vallicelliana, Rome; *Lauda spirituale* = Giancarlo Rostirolla, Danilo Zardin, and Oscar Mischiati, *La lauda spirituale tra Cinque e Seicento: Poesie e canti devozionali nell'Italia della Controriforma—Volume offerto a Giancarlo Rostirolla nel suo sessantesimo compleanno*, ed. Giuseppe Filippi et al. (Rome: Istituto di bibliografia musicale, 2001); Misch-Rost = the bibliography of laudistic collections compiled by Mischiati and Rostirolla and included in *Lauda spirituale*, pages 741–84; *ES* = Agostino Manni, *Essercitii spirituali*, 2 volumes (Brescia: Bartolomeo Fontana, 1609); *VGR* = Agostino Manni, *Valle di gigli e rose per ricreare l'anima che sta afflitta tra le spine del mondo* (Rome: Guglielmo Facciotti, at the request of Pietro Grialdi, 1619); *RVCS* = *Raccolta di versi e canzonette spirituali composte da primi Padri della Congregatione dell'Oratorio di Roma* (I-Rv, Ms. O.67).

In discussions of poetic structure, rhyme and metrical schemes are shown by means of the following system: a series of italic letters = the overall rhyme scheme; a letter in parentheses = an interior rhyme; a capital letter = a hendecasyllable line; a lowercase letter = a heptasyllable line; a lowercase letter with a ' symbol = a *tronco* line; a lowercase letter with a subscript numeral 5 = a five-syllable line.

1. *Sommo Re delle stelle*

Sommo Re delle stelle,	Divine King of stars,
Qual gran pietà ti strinse,	what a great compassion seized you,
Qual amor ti sospinse	what love pushed you
A venir giù dal cielo,	to come down from heaven,
Prender di carne il velo 5	to enter into flesh
E succhiar le mammelle	and to suck the breast
De la beata	of your blessed
Tua Genitrice amata?	and beloved Mother!
O vita, o mio ristoro,	My life, my comfort,
O speme del mio cor, t'amo e t'adoro, 10	hope of my heart, I love and worship you.
T'adoro e benedico,	I adore and bless you,
Inni e laudi ti dico,	I sing hymns and praises to you,
Unigenito Figlio,	only Begotten Son,
Che fai tremar col ciglio ogni superbo.	whose eyes make tremble all the haughty.
Tu sei del Padre il Verbo 15	You are the Word of the Father
E a la sua destra sedi	and sit on his right;
E calchi il ciel coi piedi.	the sky is under your feet.
A te mi volgo, riverente e prono:	To you I turn, reverent and prone,
Ti dimando perdono	I ask your forgiveness
E del tuo amor stupendo 20	and give eternal thanks to you
Grazie eterne ti rendo.	for your wonderful love.

Agostino Manni

Comments. The poem is arranged in prevailingly rhymed couplets of various line lengths. Other sources include *ES*, vol. 1, p. 75, and *VGR*, p. 79. *VGR* has the following variants: Line 10, entire line replaced by "luce de gli occhi, e del mio cor tesoro"; line 12, "a te" instead of "ti"; line 17 is missing. *ES* has the following variants: Line 18, "e" is inserted before "riverente;" line 19, "domando" instead of "dimando."

2. *Dal tuo volto beato*

Dal tuo volto beato	From your blessed face
Escono folgorando,	a thousand loving flames
Gesù, per ogni lato	flare out in every direction, O Jesus;
Mille fiamme d'amor, che sfavillando	their sparkling
Avampanc il mio core, 5	inflames my heart
Onde egli arde e non more.	so that it burns but does not die.
Arde il core e non more,	The heart burns but does not die,
Perché di cotal fiamma	because the more such a fire
Quanto più e più s'infiamma,	inflames it,
Tanto più si ravviva: o dolce ardore, 10	the more it revives; O sweet ardor,
Non sia mai di te privo,	may I always have you,
Ch'altramente non vivo.	otherwise I cannot live.
Altramente non vivo,	Otherwise I wouldn't be alive;
Anzi morto sarei	on the contrary, I would be dead!
E se d'altro amor vivo, 15	And if I feed on another love,
Finiscan tosto i brevi giorni miei,	may my short life end soon,
Né mi riscaldin mai	nor your burning rays
I tuoi cocenti rai.	warm me ever.
I tuoi cocenti rai	Your burning rays
Mantengon l'alma in vita, 20	keep the soul alive.
Né luce altra già mai	May no other light ever

Al mio cor sia gioconda, né gradita:
Ceda, ceda al divino
Ogni amor pellegrino.

be joyous and welcome to my heart.
May any transient love
give way to the divine love.

Comments. The poem is arranged into four hexastichic strophes. The rhyme scheme follows the same pattern in all but the second strophe: *abaBcc / cddCee / efeFgg / ghgHii*. The first line in a strophe is nearly or exactly the same as the last line in the previous strophe. At lines 12, 13, and 15, the word in rhyme has different functions (*rima equivoca*); in lines 12 and 15 "vivo" is a verb, and in line 13 it is an adjective. Other musical settings are in Misch-Rost 1591 and I-Rn, Ms. Mus. 27.

3. *Il tempo passa e mai più si ritrova*

Il tempo passa e mai più si ritrova		Time goes by and never returns,
E quel ch'ha da venir l'istesso pate;		and the future has the same fate:
Di mortal cosa non si può dar nuova,		nothing new under the sun;
Che dal tempo vien tolta in ogni etate.		time carries everything away.
Il tempo in ogni tempo il tutto accova	5	Time reaps everything at any time,
D'inverno, autunno, primavera, estate:		in winter, fall, spring, and summer.
O van desio, puro discorso umano,		O vain desire—mere human thought—
Quanto sei ingordo, inavvertito e insano!		how greedy, careless, and insane you are!
Passano i giorni e gli van dietro gli anni,		Days go by, and years follow them;
Scorron l'etadi e ci manca la vita,	10	ages glide away, and life fails us.
Non ci lascian di lor altro ch'affanni.		Nothing remains, except for troubles.
Ritardi in lungo pur la sua partita:		Even though it delays its departure,
Puro discorso uman, quanto t'inganni		O mere human thought, you are so wrong
A por le tue speranze in chi te svita!		in setting your hopes in one who carries your life away!
Ritorna in te, ritirati in disparte	15	Come to your senses, stand aloof
E volgi gli occhi ov'hai sì degna parte.		and turn your eyes to the worthy place you belong to.
Di giorno in giorno nostra vita a bada		Day after day Death keeps an eye on our life,
La Morte tiene e ci vien spesso appresso		and indeed it often comes near us.
E perché teme ognun della sua spada		Since everybody fears its sword,
Ella s'asconde e ci appresenta un messo:	20	Death hides and sends a messenger;
Il suo venire, il quando e per qual strada		when he will arrive and from which direction
Noi non sappiamo e siam cruciati spesso,		we don't know and we are often worried,
Segno che tutto il mondo in un desio		a sign that everything passes by in a moment,
Passa, eccetto ch'amar l'eterno Dio.		except for loving our eternal God.

Comment. The poem is arranged in three octaves: *ABABABCC / DEDEDEFF / GHGHGHII*.

4. *O dolce amor, Gesù*

O dolce amor, Gesù,		Jesus, sweet love,
Lo sposo mio sei tu.		you are my bridegroom.
O dolce Gesù mio,		My sweet Jesus,
La sposa tua son io.		I am your bride.
Or fammi grazia, ch'empia tuo desio	5	Grant that I may fulfill your desire
E non t'offenda più.		and not offend you any more.
Tu bianco più che giglio,		Whiter than lilies
Più di rosa vermiglio,		and more vermilion than a rose,
Il capo hai tutto d'oro.		you have a golden head.
Se non ti vedo io moro	10	If I do not see you I shall die,
E se ti vedo in croce ho gran martoro:		and if I see you on the cross, I am in great distress;
Chi mi darà consiglio?		who will give me advice?
Meglio è per te morire,		It is better to die for you
Che per altri gioire.		than to rejoice in anybody else.
Meglio è per te morire,	15	It is better to die for you
Che in altri deliziare.		than to delight in anybody else.
Dammi, Gesù, per grazia singolare		Give me, Jesus, this particular grace,
Ch'io spasmi di desire.		that I may yearn for desire.

Comments. The poem has three hexastichic strophes in the scheme *a'a'bbBa'* / *ccddDc* / *eeeFe*. The third strophe does not conform perfectly to the rhyme pattern established in the first two strophes (it should be *eeffFe*) because of an intervention probably made by the composer himself ("morire" in line 15 instead of "penare"). This text was printed for the first time in Misch-Rost 1591, p. 102 ("Anima a Gesù," see *Lauda spirituale*, pp 51 and 166–67); the lauda with the same incipit in the collection edited in Florence by Serafino Razzi (Misch-Rost 1563/1) has no other element in common with this text.

5. *Acerbe doglie e voi, piaghe amorose*

Acerbe doglie e voi, piaghe amorose,		Bitter sufferings and you, wounds caused by love,
Che nel bel corpo del mio Sposo miro,		which I contemplate in my Spouse's beautiful body,
Intorno a voi m'avvolgo e mi raggiro		I wander around you,
A guisa d'ape fra purpuree rose.		like a bee flying around purple roses.
Stillano gli occhi lagrime pietose,	5	My eyes shed compassionate tears
Mentre ch'ad una ad una vi remiro		while I stare at you, one after the other.
E dico "Ohimè,—con un dolce sospiro—		"Alas," I say in a sweet sigh.
Come fuste al mio Dio aspre e penose!"		"How bitter and painful you were to my God!"

Comments The poetic structure outlines the first half of a sonnet, in which each four-line strophe has the scheme *ABBA*. The complete sonnet appears in *RVCS*, fol. 1, where it was copied with the following variants: Line 1, "amorose" is crossed out and "formose" overwritten; line 3 has "mi volgo" instead of "m'avvolgo"; line 8, "aspre" is crossed out and "crude" overwritten. The text was printed for the first time in Misch-Rost 1591, p. 102 (see *Lauda spirituale*, pp. 51 and 113).

6. *Donna celeste, che di Dio sei Madre*

Donna celeste, che di Dio sei Madre,		Heavenly Lady, Mother of God,
Oggi al tuo parto scendon mille squadre		for your birth today a thousand crews
D'angioli santi		of holy angels are descending,
Con dolci canti:		singing sweet songs.
Maria, felice te!	5	Blissful are you, Mary!
Donna sublime, ch'hai portato in terra		Sublime Lady, you have brought on earth
La vera pace, a noi tolta hai la guerra.		true peace; you have delivered us from war.
Satan s'adira,		Satan bursts with anger;
Il ciel s'amira:		heaven admires.
Gioisca il mondo in te!	10	May the world rejoice in you!
Donna, ch'avvolgi dentro alle tue braccia		Lady, you fold in your arms
Colui che tutto l'universo abbraccia,		he who embraces all the universe,
Fatto bambino		born as a child,
E piccolino,		a little baby,
Lo stringi forte a te.	15	and you clasp him.
Donna, in cui sono tai bellezze sparse,		Lady, whose beauties are so diffused
Che 'l Verbo eterno risguardotti ed arse;		that the eternal Word looked at you and burnt,
Ora ridendo		you are now smiling
Ti stai, godendo:		and rejoicing.
Felice, dunque, te!	20	Blissful, then, are you!

Comments. The poem is arranged in four isomorphic five-line strophes with parallel rhyme schemes: AAb_5b_5x' / CCd_5d_5x' / EEf_5f_5x' / GGh_5h_5x'. The *x* represents the word "te," with which all strophes end. A number of additional musical settings are extant, including: Misch-Rost 1588/1, music by Soto de Langa (see *Lauda spirituale*, p. 136); Misch-Rost 1589/1, Soto de Langa's 1588 setting plus another text with the instruction, "cantasi come Donna celeste che di Dio sei Madre" (see *Lauda spirituale*, p. 198); Misch-Rost 1599/1, p. 24, music by Soto de Langa, for which a modern edition is available in Enrico Radesca, *Il quinto libro delle canzonette, madrigali et arie,* ed. Marco Giuliani (Lucca: Libreria musicale italiana, 2001), p. xix; Misch-Rost 1603/1, text only, to be sung on a standard aria (see *Lauda spirituale*, p. 428); Misch-Rost 1608/2, in which a new melody is presented that is probably indebted to the preexistent versions (see *Lauda spirituale*, p. 261); Misch-Rost 1614/1, a two-voice setting (see *Lauda spirituale*, pp. 250–51); Misch-

Rost 1614/2 (see *Lauda spirituale*, p. 649); Misch-Rost s.a.3 [ca. 1600–15], a three-voice setting (see *Lauda spirituale*, p. 427); Enrico Radesca, *Il quinto libro delle canzonette, madrigali et arie* (1617; modern edition by Giuliani listed above); Misch-Rost 1621–22 (see *Lauda spirituale*, p. 649); Misch-Rost 1634 (see *Lauda spirituale*, p. 649); Misch-Rost 1657/2 (see *Lauda spirituale*, p. 649). Other laudistic collections contain only the text: Misch-Rost 1603/2 (see *Lauda spirituale*, p. 426); Misch-Rost 1621/1 (see *Lauda spirituale*, pp. 414 and 444); Misch-Rost 1654/1 (see *Lauda spirituale*, p. 428); Misch-Rost 1660 (see *Lauda spirituale*, p. 429); Misch-Rost 1660–66 (see *Lauda spirituale*, p. 429).

7. *La matutina aurora*

La matutina aurora	Morning dawn
Già d'ogni intorno indora	is already touching everything around with gold;
E fa mormorar l'onde	it allows the waves to murmur
E tremolar le fronde.	and the foliage to tremble.
Sopra de gli arboscelli 5	It lets the lovely birds
Fa che i vezzosi augelli	sing sweetly
Cantin soavemente	in the saplings
E rida l'oriente.	and the Orient smile.
Ecco che l'alba appare	Here dawn appears;
E si specchia nel mare 10	it mirrors itself in the sea;
E rasserena il cielo,	it makes the sky serene
Già coperto di gelo.	that was covered with cold before.
Ognun corra a vederla,	Everybody should come to see it
Ch'ogni campagna imperla	while it pearls the countryside
E col soffiar del'aura 15	and restores every heart
Ogni arso cor ristaura.	with its breeze.

Comment. The poem is arranged in four quatrains of heptasyllables with parallel rhyme schemes: *aabb / ccdd / eeff / gghh*.

8. *Ecco riede, ecco soggiorna*

Ecco riede, ecco soggiorna	Here it comes again, here it dwells:
Primavera vaga, adorna	spring, charming and florid,
E predice e manifesta	predicts and reveals
Come amor seco si desta.	how love awakes with it.
Ecco scaccia il verno e toglie 5	Here spring sends winter away and satisfies
Primavera le sue voglie	its own desires;
E le più ruzzute piante	the most frozen plants
Tornan vive al suo sembiante.	revive in its presence.
Ecco i prati e gli arboscelli	Here meadows and saplings
Verdeggianti si fan belli 10	are turning green and beautiful,
E di coloriti fiori	and of colorful flowers
Primavera dà gli odori.	spring spreads the scent.
Ecco i monti alpestri e i mari,	Here mountains and seas
Tutti ombrosi e d'acque chiari,	are all shadowy and with limpid waters,
E gli augelli in mille modi 15	and birds, in many ways,
Danno a primavera lodi.	give praise unto spring.

Comments. The poem is arranged in four quatrains of octosyllables with parallel rhyme schemes: *aabb / ccdd / eeff / gghh*. Another musical setting is in British Library, Add. 36877 ("Villanelle di più sorte con l'intavolatura per sonare et cantare su la chitarra alla spagnola di Giovanni Casalotti"), fols. 105–105v; see the catalogue in John Walter Hill, *Roman Monody, Cantata, and Opera from the Circles around Cardinal Montalto*, 2 vols. (Oxford: Clarendon Press, 1997), 1:399.

9. *Pulchra es*

Pulchra es, amica mea, et macula non est in te. Veni de Libano, speciosa mea, veni, coronaberis; de capite Aman, de cubilibus leonum, de montibus pardorum. Vulnerasti

You are fair, my love; there is no spot on you. Come from Lebanon, my sweetheart, come, you will be crowned, from the top of Aman, from the dens of lions, from the

cor meum in uno oculorum tuorum, et in uno crine colli tui. Quam pulchrae sunt mammae tuae! Pulchriora sunt ubera tua vino, et odor unguentorum tuorum super omnia aromata.

Comment. Based on Song of Songs 4:7–10.

mountains of leopards. You have ravished my heart with one of your eyes, with one of your curls. How fair are your breasts! How much better is your bosom than wine, and the fragrance of your oils than any spice!

10. *Veni sponsa Christi*

Veni sponsa Christi, accipe coronam, quam tibi Dominus praeparavit in aeternum.

Comment. Antiphon from the Common of Virgins.

Come, bride of Christ, receive the crown that the Lord has prepared for you forever.

11. *Regina caeli*

Regina caeli laetare, alleluia:
Quia quem meruisti portare, alleluia:
Resurrexit, sicut dixit, alleluia:
Ora pro nobis Deum, alleluia.

Comment. Marian antiphon.

O Queen of heaven, rejoice, alleluia,
for he whom you did merit to bear, alleluia,
has arisen as he said, alleluia!
Pray for us to God, alleluia.

12. *Ego flos campi*

Ego flos campi, et lilium convallium. Sicut lilium inter spinas, sic amica mea inter filias. Sicut malum inter ligna silvarum, sic dilectus meus inter filios. Sub umbra illius quem desideraveram sedi, et fructus eius dulcis gutturi meo.

Comment. Based on Song of Songs 2:1–3.

I am the flower of the field and the lily of the valleys. As the lily among thorns, so is my love among maidens. As the apple tree among the trees of the wood, so is my beloved among young men. I sat under his shadow with great delight, and his fruit was sweet to my taste.

13. *Salve, Regina*

Salve, Regina, Mater misericordiae: vita, dulcedo, et spes nostra, salve. Ad te clamamus, exsules filii Hevae. Ad te suspiramus, gementes et flentes in hac lacrimarum valle. Eia ergo, Advocata nostra, illos tuos misericordes oculos ad nos converte. Et Jesum, benedictum fructum ventris tui, nobis post hoc exsilium ostende. O clemens: o pia: o dulcis Virgo Maria.

Comment. Marian antiphon.

Hail, Queen, Mother of mercy, our life, our sweetness, and our hope. To you do we cry, poor banished children of Eve. To you do we send up our sighs, mourning and weeping in this valley of tears. Turn then, most gracious Advocate, your eyes of mercy toward us. And after this our exile show unto us the blessed fruit of your womb, Jesus. O merciful, O loving, O sweet Virgin Mary.

14. *Salve Regina, Madre divina*

Salve Regina,		Hail, Queen,
Madre divina,		Mother of God,
Dolce e gradita,		sweet and pleasant,
Mia speme e vita;		my hope and life.
Io che sbandito	5	I am banished,
Sono, e smarrito		I have lost
Ho il dritto calle,		the right path;
Per questa valle		in this valley,
Pien di martiro		sorrowful,
Piango e sospiro	10	I weep and sigh,
E a te rivolto		and I turn to you
Ho il core e il volto.		my heart and face.
O dolce e pia		O my sweet
Signora mia.		and pious Lady,
O mia avvocata	15	O my holy
Santa e beata,		and blessed Advocate,
Quegli occhi tuoi		by your faith,
Santi, se vuoi,		if you wish,
Per la tua fé		turn towards me
Rivolgi a me	20	your holy eyes,

E doppo questa		and after this
Stanza molesta		troublesome stay
Del tuo bel Figlio		show me
Bianco e vermiglio		in heaven
Nel paradiso	25	the white and vermilion
Mostrami il viso.		face of your Child.

Agostino Manni

Comments. The poem is arranged in rhymed couplets of five-syllable lines. Other sources include *ES,* vol. 1, p. 87 and *VGR,* p. 433. *VGR* has the following variants: Line 12, "flebil" instead of "core e il"; line 14, "Regina" instead of "Signora"; line 18, "Dolci" instead of "Santi"; line 20, "Rivolta" instead of "Rivolgi"; "Amen" is added after the last line.

15. *Gesù, nel tuo partire*

ANIMA
Gesù, nel tuo partire
Io mi sento morire.

CRISTO
Se tu m'amassi, sposa,
Tutta lieta e gioiosa
Saresti, essendo ch'io   5
Or vado al Padre mio.

ANIMA
Del tuo sublime onore
Gioisco, almo Signore,
Ma come voi ch'io viva,
Se di te, amor, son priva?   10

CRISTO
Meco sempre star puoi,
Anima, se tu vuoi.

ANIMA
Questo pur mi consola,
Se ben rimang'or sola;
Ma 'l mondo non intende come sia   15
Che partendo tu, dolce vita mia,
Io teco sempre stia.

CRISTO
Nella mia bella imago
L'occhio di mirar vago
Prenderà tal diletto   20
Qual non cape intelletto.

ANIMA
Ma quando fia quel giorno
Ch'io miri il viso adorno?
Sposo diletto e caro,
A me par troppo amaro   25
Mancar della tua vista,
La cui forza conquista
Ogni rubello core:
Pur da me fuggi, amore!

SOUL
Jesus, while you are leaving
I feel I am dying.

CHRIST
If you loved me, my spouse,
you would be happy and joyful,
since I am now going
to my Father.

SOUL
For your high honor
I rejoice, noble Lord,
but how can you expect me to live,
if I am deprived of you, my love?

CHRIST
You can always stay with me,
soul, if you like.

SOUL
This comforts me,
though now I am left alone.
But the world doesn't understand
how it can be that I will always stay with you,
even if you, my sweet life, are leaving.

CHRIST
Your eyes, eager to contemplate,
will be delighted
in my beautiful image,
more than intellect can comprehend.

SOUL
But when will that day come
when I will look at your handsome face?
My beloved and dear spouse,
it seems to me too bitter
to be deprived of your visible presence,
whose strength conquers
every rebellious heart;
however, flee from me, my love!

Comments. The poem is arranged in prevailingly rhymed couplets of various line lengths. Another musical setting is in Misch-Rost 1591 ("Nell'Ascensione del Signore," a three-voice setting; see *Lauda spirituale,* p. 141). In Anerio's musical setting, the second voice sings along with the first from line 24 to the end, although these words pertain logically to Anima alone in the dialogue.

16. *Ecco che i monti indora*

Ecco che i monti indora		Here's morning dawn
La matutina aurora:		touching the mountains with gold;
Cor mio, con l'occhio interno		my heart, with your internal eye,
Contempla il Sol eterno.		contemplate the eternal Sun.
Mira la sua gradita	5	Look at his pleasing
Luce, che dà la vita,		light, which gives life.
Mira la sua bellezza		Look at his beauty
E ogni altra cosa sprezza.		and despise anything else.
O Padre alto dei lumi,		O high Father of the stars,
Sian puri i miei costumi	10	let my morals be pure
E accendi nel mio core		and light the fire of love
La fiamma dell'amore.		in my heart.
Fammi veder ch'è vana		Let me see how vain
Ogni grandezza umana		is human greatness,
E che 'l tempo che passa	15	and that time, as it passes,
Tutte l'altezze abbassa.		brings every height low.
Al Padre e al Figlio sia		Power and lordship be
Imperio e signoria,		to the Father and the Son,
Ed al divin Amore		and eternal honor be
Sia sempiterno onore.	20	to the Holy Spirit.

                     Agostino Manni

Comments. The poem is arranged in five quatrains of heptasyllables with parallel rhyme schemes: *aabb / ccdd / eeff / gghh / iiff* (the third and fifth quatrains end in the same syllable). Other sources are *ES*, vol. 1, p. 40, and *VGR*, p. 381. Line 11 in *VGR* omits "E." Line 17 in *ES* omits "e." A musical setting by Felice Anerio is in I-Rv Ms. Z. 122–30.

17. *Alta cosa è il mio Dio*

Alta cosa è il mio Dio,		My God is high;
Alto e di gloria pieno è il Signor mio.		high and full of glory is my Lord.
O genti, come è buono e come è grande		O people, how good and magnificent
Il gran Signor delle virtù mirande!		is the great Lord whose powers are admirable!
Ma non è buono il mio Signore,	5	But my Lord is good
Se non a gente che ha retto il cuore.		only to right-hearted people.
Udite, o cieli,		Listen, O heavens,
Levate i veli		raise the veils
E a noi mostrate		and show us
La Deitate!	10	the Divinity!
Ma non si può mirar tanto splendore,		But you cannot look at such a splendor
Se non luce nel cor luce d'amore.		if the light of love does not shine in your heart.
Sta con noi chi fé noi, né se n'avvede		Our Creator stays with us,
Il cuor che non ha fede.		but the unfaithful heart does not realize it.
O maraviglia eterna!	15	O eternal wonder!
La Maiestà superna		The celestial Majesty
Di starsi sempre ha stabilito il patto		elected to remain forever
Con le cose create che ella ha fatto.		with his own creatures.
Il mio Dio sta nascosto		My God remains hidden;
E 'l luoco suo dentro a le cose ha posto.	20	he set his place amidst his creation.
Sta il mio Signor secreto		My Lord is concealed,
E nei riposi suoi giace quieto		he lays quietly in his rest.
E, mentre stassi agli occhi nostri ignoto,		And while he remains invisible to our eyes,
Dona a le cose sue la vita e 'l moto.		he gives life and motion to his creatures.
O cuori, udite,	25	Listen, O hearts,
Cuori, stupite:		and wonder:
Il Signor che è con meco e con esso io		the Lord who is with me, and I with him,
È sommo, eterno e incomprensibil Dio.		is the highest, eternal, incomprehensible God.

                     Agostino Manni

Comments. The poem is arranged in a heterometric series of rhymed couplets. Line 5 is hypometric, unless a highly improbable combined use of *dialepha* (between "buono" and "il") and diaeresis ("mïo") is considered. *VGR* (see below) emends this lacuna. Other sources are *ES,* vol. 2, p. 149, and *VGR,* p. 39. *VGR* has the following variants: Line 3, "o come" instead of "e come"; line 5, "dolce" is inserted between "mio" and "Signore" to correct the hypometric syllable count; line 6, "genti ch'hanno" instead of "gente che ha"; line 20, "luogo" instead of "luoco"; line 27, "sta meco" instead of "è con meco."

18. Ecco vien fuor la notte

Ecco vien fuor la notte	Here comes the night
Da le profonde grotte:	out of the deep caverns.
Voi, del ciel Luce eterna,	You, eternal Light of the sky,
Siate al mio cor lucerna,	be a lantern to my heart,
Acciò ch'in mezzo all'ombre 5	so that amidst the nocturnal shadows
Notturne non m'ingombre	my fierce enemy
Di tenebre il pensiero	will not fill
Il mio nemico fiero.	my thoughts with darkness.
Venite, alto Signore,	Come, high Lord,
In guardia del mio core, 10	to guard my heart,
Perché non sia gravato	so that it will not be burdened
Dal sonno del peccato,	by the sleep of sin.
Ché, doppo il mio riposo,	Then, after my rest,
Nel giorno luminoso	in the shining daylight,
Dirò con lieto core 15	I will sing with joyful heart
Un inno in vostro onore.	a hymn in your honor.

Agostino Manni

Comments. The poem is arranged in four quatrains of heptasyllables with parallel rhyme schemes: *aabb / ccdd / eeff / ggee* (the same rhyme appears, in different positions, in the third and fourth quatrains). Other sources are *ES,* vol. 1, p. 26, and *VGR,* p. 380. Line 12 in *VGR* has "Col" instead of "Dal."

19. Occhi del cielo ardenti

Occhi del cielo ardenti,	Burning eyes of the sky,
Vaghe stelle lucenti,	beautiful shining stars,
Vagheggiose e serene,	charming and serene,
Fatevi tutte piene	shine in your full splendor
E sopra il proprio manto 5	and burn in the most proud way
Ardete altiere tanto	in your mantle of light,
Alla venuta ch'ora	since dawn is coming
Fa nel mondo l'aurora.	to the world.
Sian con i vostri lumi	May your light
Scoperti i suoi costumi: 10	reveal its deeds:
Ch'a l'un e l'altro polo	how dawn spreads out suddenly
Ella si stende a volo	from one pole to the other;
E seco coi bei raggi	how the sun moves along,
Il sol fa i suoi viaggi,	with beautiful sunbeams,
Per riportar vittoria 15	to carry off the victory
Di sua dovuta gloria.	of its rightful glory.
Nel ciel lucenti stelle,	Stars shining in the sky,
Fatevi tutte belle,	make yourself pretty
Quando l'alba celeste	when the celestial dawn
Il real manto veste, 20	puts on its regal mantle,
Acciò che d'ogni intorno	so that the day may be clearly seen
Si veda chiaro il giorno	from everywhere,
E renda ogni paese	and every country become
Al suo venir cortese.	courteous by its coming.

Comment. The poem is arranged in three strophes of heptasyllables with parallel rhyme schemes: *aabbccdd / eeffgghh / iijjkkll*.

20. *Alzate al sommo ciel memoria e mente*

Alzate al sommo ciel memoria e mente,	Raise your memory and mind to the highest sky,
Cuor, lingua, i suoni e i pronti affetti unite	join your heart, tongue, voice, and immediate sentiments
E l'altissimo Re del ciel lucente,	and bless the highest King of the bright heaven,
E 'l fabbro delle stelle luminose,	the maker of the shining stars,
Che fé tutte le cose, benedite. 5	who created everything.
Sia benedetta	Blessed be
La Trinità perfetta,	the perfect Trinity
Che sopra i cieli sta	that is over the heavens
Con gloria e maiestà	in its glory and majesty
E gloriosa e degna 10	and, glorious and dignified,
Vive beata e regna.	reigns and lives in beatitude.
Sia benedetto il Padre	Blessed be the Father
Da le celesti squadre,	by the celestial crews,
Sia il Figlio benedetto	blessed be the Son
Dal suo popolo eletto 15	by his chosen people;
E il santo Spirto benedetto sia,	and blessed be the Holy Spirit
Che col Padre e col Figlio ha signoria.	that is Lord with the Father and the Son.
Sia benedetta ancora	Blessed be also
Maria, splendor del ciel, candida aurora,	Mary, splendor of heaven, spotless dawn,
Che sotto il piede tien la luna aurata, 20	who holds the resplendent moon under her feet
Di stelle incoronata.	and is crowned with stars.
Sian benedetti	Blessed be
Gli angeli eletti	the noble angels
Con inni e canti;	with hymns and songs;
Sian benedetti i santi. 25	blessed be the saints.
E voi, Re delle genti,	And you, King of the nations,
E voi, Regina mia,	and you, my Queen,
Con gli angeli lucenti,	together with the shining angels
Coi santi in compagnia	and with the saints,
Benedite dal ciel la mente e 'l core 30	bless from heaven the mind and heart
Che benedice in terra il mio Signore.	that bless my Lord on earth.
E voi, genti disperse	And you, nations scattered
Dove sorgono i monti e giran l'onde,	where the mountains rise and the sea is rough,
Al ciel converse,	turning to heaven
Liete e gioconde, 35	joyous and cheerful,
Come laudo io,	as I praise him,
Benedite l'altissimo Re mio.	bless my highest King.
Inno gioconcio	Jocund hymn,
Sia al Re del mondo,	be to the King of the world
Inno con canto 40	a hymn with a celestial
Celeste e santo,	and holy song,
Canto con salmi, salmi e laudi eterne,	a song with psalms, psalms and eternal praises,
Con voci alterne,	alternating the voices
Con terse note e con sonante verso	with clear tones and sonorous verse:
Dica ogni lingua al Re dell'universo. 45	this every tongue should say to the King of the universe!

Agostino Manni

Comments The poem is arranged in seven heterometric strophes with varying rhyme schemes: *ABAC(c)B / d₅de'e'ff / gghhII / jJKk / l₅l₅m₅mniniOO / pQp₅q₅r₅R / s₅s₅t₅t₅Uu₅VV*. Other sources are *ES*, vol. 2, p. 137, and *VGR*, p. 38. *VGR* has the following variants: Line 1, "Alzati" instead of "Alzate"; line 13, "Dalle" instead of "Da le"; lines 14–15 are reversed, and line 14 (= 15) has "E dal" instead of "Dal suo"; line 19 is replaced with "Maria Madre di Dio del ciel Signora"; line 20, "i piedi" instead of "il piede"; line 41, "Sia al Re che è santo" instead of "Celeste e santo"; line 42 inserts "e" between "salmi" and "salmi." Line 14 in *ES* has "Sii" instead of "Sia."

21. Torna la sera bruna

Torna la sera bruna
E in ciel luce la luna,
Che 'l mortal egro invita
Al sonno della vita.

Salva me, Signor forte, 5
Dal sonno della morte
E stammi sempre intorno,
Sinché ritorni il giorno.

Mentre mi stai presente
Fugga via incontinente 10
Innanzi al tuo splendore
La tenebra e l'orrore.

Fammi, Signor diletto,
Dormir sopra il tuo petto
E notte e giorno stia 15
Con te la vita mia.

Sia laude, gloria e canto
Al Padre, al Figlio e al santo
Spirto, che 'l ciel governa
Con legge sempiterna. 20

Agostino Manni

The dark eventide returns
and the moon shines in the sky,
inviting the afflicted mortals
to their natural sleep.

Save me, mighty Lord,
from the sleep of death,
and stay close by me
until daylight comes back.

As long as you are near,
in front of your splendor
may darkness and horror
run away immediately.

My dear Lord,
let me sleep upon your breast,
and may I spend my life
with you night and day.

Praise, glory, and singing
be to the Father, the Son,
and the Holy Spirit, who rule heaven
with everlasting law.

Comments. The poem is arranged in five quatrains of heptasyllables with parallel rhyme schemes: *aabb / ccdd / eeff / gghh / iijj*. Other sources are *ES*, vol. 1, p. 52, and *VGR*, p. 380. Line 16 in *VGR* has "quest'alma" instead of "la vita." A musical setting by Felice Anerio is in I-Rv Ms. Z. 122–30.

22. Dio ti salvi, Maria, Madre divina

Dio ti salvi, Maria, Madre divina,
Degli angeli Regina;
Dio ti salvi, Maria, stella serena,
Di luce e gloria piena.
Vergine eterna, Madre dell'amore, 5
Con teco è il tuo Signore.
Benedetta sii tu
E il tuo Figliol dolcissimo Gesù.
Santa Maria,
Speranza mia, 10
Madre di Dio,
Refugio mio,
Prega il Signor per me,
Prega per me, Signora,
Or ch'ho bisogno e nella morte ancora. 15
Così sia, così sia,
Dolce vergine Maria.

Agostino Manni

Hail Mary, divine Mother,
Queen of the angels.
Hail Mary, serene star,
full of light and glory.
Eternal Virgin, Mother of love,
your Lord is with you.
Be blessed, you
and your most sweet Son, Jesus.
Holy Mary,
my hope,
Mother of God,
my refuge,
pray to the Lord for me,
pray for me, Lady,
now that I am in need and at my death's door.
Amen, amen,
sweet Virgin Mary!

Comments. The poem is arranged in prevailingly rhymed couplets of various line lengths. Another source is *ES*, vol. 1, p. 97, in which line 15 has "che ho" instead of "ch'ho." A musical setting of a poem with the same incipit appears in the Florentine *Laudario* (1721), fols. 60–60v (see *Lauda spirituale*, p. 547).

23. O tu, che vai per via

ANIMA
O tu, che vai per via,
Dimmi per cortesia:
Chi sei? chi cercar tenti
Con tanti tuoi spaventi?

SOUL
You, going along the way,
please, tell me:
who are you? Whom are you looking for
with such frightful actions?

MORTE
Son Morte.

ANIMA
Or che vuoi, di'?

MORTE
Tua vita.

ANIMA
Eccola qui.

MORTE
Oggi non la vogl'io.

ANIMA
Pigliala a tuo desio:
Già fatto ho provisione.

MORTE
Dove?

ANIMA
Nella magione
Del cielo.

MORTE
E chi ci hai tu?

ANIMA
La Madre di Gesù.

MORTE
E per qual merto l'hai?

ANIMA
Ho sol lodato i rai
Di sua eccellenza e poi
Servito a i voler suoi.
Ma tu, ch'ognor mi chiami,
Altro da me più brami?

MORTE
Il fin della tua vita.

ANIMA
Il fin della mia vita
Ottenerlo non puoi.

MORTE
Ed a chi darla vuoi?

ANIMA
A quel ch'è vita eterna
Di gloria sempiterna.

MORTE
Non è commun editto,
Ch'ognun da me sia afflitto?

ANIMA
Sì, ma non sempre a un modo.

VITA
Che sento, vedo ed odo?
Morte, non ha condegno
Quest'alma del tuo regno
E, perché Dio m'addita
Ch'io venga a dargli vita,

DEATH
5   I am Death.

SOUL
Tell me: what do you want?

DEATH
I want your life.

SOUL
Here you are.

DEATH
Today I don't want it.

SOUL
Take it, if you like;
I have already provided for myself.

DEATH
10   Where?

SOUL
In the house
of heaven.

DEATH
And who is there to help you?

SOUL
The Mother of Jesus.

DEATH
And by which merit?

SOUL
I only praised
15   her bright excellence
and then served under her will.
But you, calling on me every now and then,
what else do you want from me?

DEATH
The end of your life.

SOUL
20   The end of my life
you cannot obtain.

DEATH
And to whom will you give it?

SOUL
To whom is eternal life
in everlasting glory.

DEATH
25   Is it not a common law
that everybody should be afflicted by me?

SOUL
Yes, but not always in the same way.

LIFE
What do I hear and see?
Death, this soul does not deserve
30   to enter your reign,
and since God has entrusted me
to come and give it life,

Meco essergli consorte		come and escort it with me
Sin a del ciel le porte.		up to the doors of heaven.
MORTE		DEATH
Da poi che so' interdetta,	35	Since I am deprived of my rights,
Faccia quel fin ch'aspetta:		let it have the fate it deserves.
Teco al celeste coro		I will bring it with you
Vuo' recondurla.		to the heavenly choir.
ANIMA		SOUL
Moro!		I die!
CORO		CHOIR
Vieni, anima beata,		Come, blessed soul,
Colombella d'amore,	40	little dove of love,
Vien, che sei esaltata		come, now that you are exalted
Dall'eterno Signore.		by the eternal Lord!

Comment. The poem is arranged in rhymed couplets of heptasyllables with a final quatrain rhyming *abab*.

24. *O del gran Redentor Madre alma e bella*

O del gran Redentor Madre alma e bella,		Noble and beautiful Mother of the great Redeemer,
Porta del ciel lucente,		shining portal of the sky,
O del mar fiero avventurosa stella,		fortunate star of the wild sea,
Con la virtù divina		by the divine virtue
Della tua man potente	5	of your mighty hand,
Soccorri alla ruina		help the ruined
Della smarrita gente,		and lost people
Che cade e mercé grida		who, sinking, call for aid
E solo in te si fida.		and trust only you;
Tu che, nel fior primiero,	10	you, who heard in your youth
Del sopran messaggero		the sweet news of our salvation
Felice udisti quella		brought by the celestial messenger,
Dolce salute, amata verginella,		you, beloved Virgin,
E più d'ogni altra pura,		most pure among women.
Con stupor di natura,	15	To the wonderment of nature,
Vergine innanzi al sacro parto e poi,		Virgin before the sacred birth and after,
Hai generato a noi		for us you begot
Il Verbo sempiterno,		the everlasting Word,
Signor del ciel superno:		the supernal Lord of heaven.
Abbraccia i peccatori	20	Embrace the sinners
Coi tuoi beati amori.		with your blessed love!

Agostino Manni

Comments. The poem is arranged in a free series of hendecasyllables and heptasyllables, with a prevalence of rhymed couplets. Other sources are *ES*, vol. 1, p. 75, and *VGR*, p. 424. *VGR* has the following variants: Line 3, "E" instead of "O"; line 18, "Genitor eterno" instead of "Verbo sempiterno." A musical setting by Felice Anerio is in I-Rv Ms. Z. 122–130; Felice sets a distinct version of the text that may be derived from the sketches in I-Rv Ms. O.68 (fols. 189–90).

25. *Ave Maria, Speranza mia*

Ave Maria,		Hail Mary,
Speranza mia,		my hope,
Stella serena,		clear star,
Di grazia piena;		full of grace,
Dio mio Signore	5	God, my Lord,
Sta nel tuo core.		is in your heart.
O te beata,		Blessed are you
Tra l'altre nata!		among women
Sia benedetto		and blessed is
Il tuo diletto	10	your beloved

Gesù, mia vita,		Jesus, my life
Bontà infinita.		and infinite goodness.
Madre di Dio,		Mother of God,
Conforto mio,		my consolation,
Prega il Signore	15	pray to the Lord
Che per tuo amore		that for your sake
Aprir mi faccia		he let me,
Con lieta faccia,		with benevolent countenance,
Doppo la morte,		through the doors of heaven
Del ciel le porte.	20	after my death.

Agostino Manni

Comments. The poem is arranged in rhymed couplets of five-syllable lines. Other sources are *ES,* vol. 1, p. 61, and *VGR,* p. 424. *VGR* has the following variants: Line 12, "Beltà" instead of "Bontà"; line 14, "Refugio" instead of "Conforto." Another musical setting is in Misch-Rost 1614/1 (a two-voice setting; see *Lauda spirituale*, p. 250).

26. *Io non saprei dir quanto*

Io non saprei dir quanto		I cannot say how much
Prende il mio cor diletto		delight my heart receives
Da quel soave canto,		in the sweet singing
Che manda fuor dal petto		that my dear Cicada
La mia cara Cicala, le cui note	5	utters out of her chest.
Cigno o sirena pareggiar non pote.		Neither a swan nor a siren could equal her notes.
Il ciel corona pose		Heaven put a crown
Nella regal sua testa,		on her regal head,
Non di caduche rose,		made not out of transient roses,
Ma di rubin contesta,	10	but of rubies;
Ond'a lei nel cantar com'a regina		therefore, as to singing, every bird is silent,
Ogni augel col tacer cede e s'inchina.		giving up and bowing to her as to a queen.
Ella si reca a sdegno		She disdains
Di salutar l'aurora		to hail the dawn
E l'aura, che col giorno	15	and the breeze coming up
Dal mar escono fuora;		from the sea with the daylight.
Solo saluta il sol e vol ch'i venti		She greets only the sun and wants the
Tacciano al suon de' suoi soavi accenti.		winds to be silent while her sweet notes resonate.
Ella gli agricoltori		She calls the farmers
Chiama con certa spene	20	with a certain hope,
E ne gli estivi ardori		and in the summer heat
Col canto gl'intrattiene,		she entertains them, singing,
Promettendo ad ognor di render loro		always promising to give them back
Nelle dorate spighe il secol d'oro.		the golden age through the golden spikes.
È ver ch'in terra nasce,	25	It is true that she is born on the earth,
Ma non ha sangue e solo		but she has no blood
Di rugiada si pasce;		and she feeds only on dew.
Da lei fugge ogni dolo:		Every malice shuns away from her.
Vive senza timor, solo ha di male		She lives free from fears; her only fault
Che mostra col morir d'esser mortale.	30	is that, dying, she shows her mortal nature.
Il mondo, dunque, avampi,		May, then, the world be inflamed
Purché tu canti sempre,		as long as you sing forever,
Sirenetta de' campi;		O little mermaid of the fields.
Ch'udendo le tue tempre		To listen to the timbre of your voice
Parmi d'udir temprar al dio di Delo	35	seems to me to hear the god of Delos
Il canto suo con l'armonia del cielo.		blending his singing with the harmony of heaven.

Comments. The poem is arranged in six isomorphic strophes with parallel rhyme schemes: *aabbCC / ddeeFF / ghghII / jkjkLL / mnmnOO / pqpqRR*. In the third strophe (lines 13–15), the imperfect rhyme between "sdegno" and "giorno" (partial graphic consonance and assonance) is probably caused by an alteration of the original text (possibly "sdegno" instead of "scorno," "giorno" instead of "legno," or the like).

27. *Litaniae Beatae Mariae Virginis*

Kyrie eleison.	Lord, have mercy on us.
Christe eleison.	Christ, have mercy on us.
Kyrie eleison.	Lord, have mercy on us.
Pater de caelis Deus, miserere nobis.	God the Father of heaven, have mercy on us.
Fili Redemptor mundi Deus, miserere nobis.	God the Son, Redeemer of the world, have mercy on us.
Spiritus sancte Deus, miserere nobis.	God the Holy Spirit, have mercy on us.
Sancta Trinitas unus Deus, miserere nobis.	Holy Trinity, one God, have mercy on us.
Sancta Maria, ora pro nobis.	Holy Mary, pray for us.
Sancta Dei Genitrix, ora pro nobis.	Holy Mother of God, pray for us.
Sancta Virgo Virginum, ora pro nobis.	Holy Virgin of Virgins, pray for us.
Mater Christi, ora pro nobis.	Mother of Christ, pray for us.
Mater divinae gratiae, ora pro nobis.	Mother of divine grace, pray for us.
Mater purissima, ora pro nobis.	Mother most pure, pray for us.
Mater castissima, ora pro nobis.	Mother most chaste, pray for us.
Mater inviolata, ora pro nobis.	Mother inviolate, pray for us.
Mater intemerata, ora pro nobis.	Mother undefiled, pray for us.
Mater admirabilis, ora pro nobis.	Mother most admirable, pray for us.
Virgo veneranda et praedicanda, ora pro nobis.	Virgin most venerable and renowned, pray for us.
Virgo prudentissima, ora pro nobis.	Virgin most prudent, pray for us.
Sedes sapientiae, ora pro nobis.	Seat of wisdom, pray for us.
Causa nostrae laetitiae, ora pro nobis.	Cause of our joy, pray for us.
Domus aurea, ora pro nobis.	House of gold, pray for us.
Stella matutina, ora pro nobis.	Morning star, pray for us.
Salus infirmorum, ora pro nobis.	Health of the sick, pray for us.
Refugium peccatorum, ora pro nobis.	Refuge of sinners, pray for us.
Consolatrix afflictorum, ora pro nobis.	Comforter of the afflicted, pray for us.
Auxilium Christianorum, ora pro nobis.	Helper of Christians, pray for us.
Regina Angelorum, ora pro nobis.	Queen of angels, pray for us.
Regina Patriarcharum et Prophetarum, ora pro nobis.	Queen of patriarchs and prophets, pray for us.
Regina Apostolorum, ora pro nobis.	Queen of apostles, pray for us.
Regina Martyrum et Confessorum, ora pro nobis.	Queen of martyrs and confessors, pray for us.
Regina Virginum, ora pro nobis.	Queen of virgins, pray for us.
Regina Sanctorum omnium, ora pro nobis.	Queen of all saints, pray for us.
Agnus Dei, qui tollis peccata mundi, parce nobis Domine.	Lamb of God, who takes away the sins of the world, spare us, O Lord.
Agnus Dei, qui tollis peccata mundi, exaudi nos Domine.	Lamb of God, who takes away the sins of the world, graciously hear us, O Lord.
Agnus Dei, qui tollis peccata mundi, miserere nobis.	Lamb of God, who takes away the sins of the world, have mercy on us.

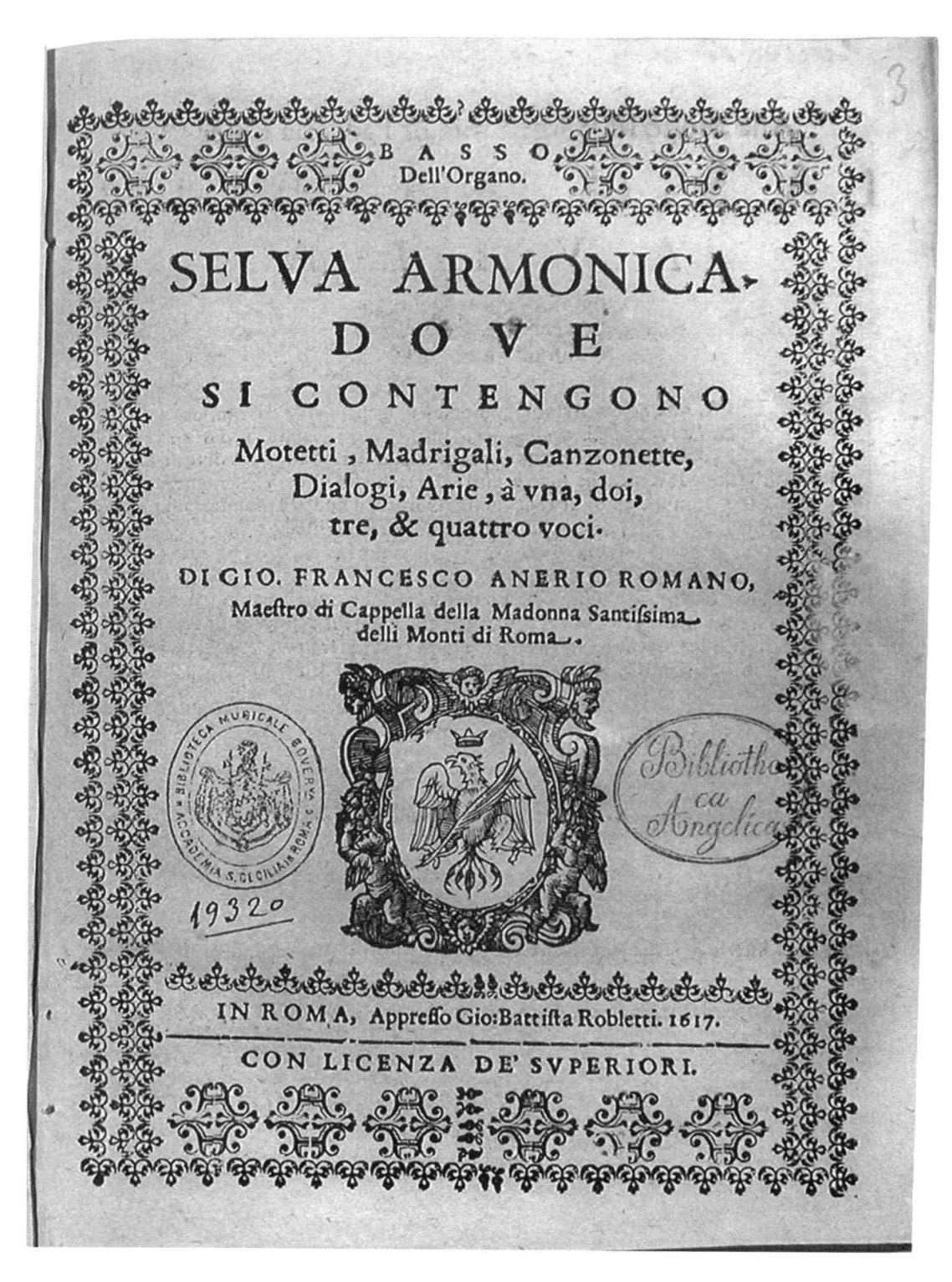

Plate 1. Giovanni Francesco Anerio, *Selva armonica* (Rome, 1617), title page from the Basso dell'organo partbook. Courtesy of the Biblioteca del Conservatorio di Santa Cecilia, Rome.

Alla Molto Ill.re Sig.ra mia, & Padrona Osser.ma

LA SIG. ISABELLA AVILA

A mia Selua Armonica non ho voluto sia vista dal mondo sotto altro nome, che di quello, al cui intuito, & richiesta in diuersi tempi ho composto, in occasioni parimente diuerse, che però diuerse sono anco le opre, che sono in esa. La richiesta fù di V. S. mentre li dauo lettione di Musica, & questa mi spinse à punto à mandarla fuori freggiata del nome suo; per far conoscere nell'istesso tempo, & à lei & alli Signori suo Padre, & Madre la memoria, che tengo de fauori continui, che riceuo da casa loro. M'assicuro, che gradirà V. S. il dono, come io riceuei volentieri il carico di dare alle Stampe queste mie fatiche, quali accompagnarò al suo tempo con altre per aumentarli tuttauia maggiormente il desiderio di far maggior profitto nella Musica, come ha fatto fin qui in età così tenera con tanto gusto e de suoi genitori, & mio insieme. & le bacio le mani. Di Roma il di 10. Agosto. 1617.

Di V. S. Molto Illustre.

Affettionatissimo seruitore

Gio. Francesco Anerio.

Imprimatur, si placet Reuerendiss. P. M. S. P. Apost. Caesar Fidelis. Vicesg.

Imprimatur, Fr. Gregorjus Donatus Reuerendiss. P. M. S. P. Apost. Socius

Plate 2. Giovanni Francesco Anerio, *Selva armonica* (Rome, 1617), dedication from the Canto partbook. Courtesy of the Biblioteca del Conservatorio di Santa Cecilia, Rome.

Plate 3. Giovanni Francesco Anerio, *Selva armonica* (Rome, 1617), first page of "Sommo Re delle stelle" (no. 1) from the Canto partbook. Courtesy of the Biblioteca del Conservatorio di Santa Cecilia, Rome.

TAVOLA.

A VNA VOCE.

Tutte queste si possono cantare in Soprano, & in Tenore.

Sommo Rè dlle stelle.	3
Dal tuo volto. Prima parte.	5
Arde il Core. Seconda parte.	5
Altramente. Terza parte.	6
I tuoi cocenti rai. Quarta parte.	7
Il tempo passa. Prima parte.	8
Passano i giorni. Seconda parte.	9
Di giorno in giorno. Terza, & Vlt. Par.	10
O dolce amor Giesù. Prima parte.	11
Tu bianco. Seconda parte.	12
Meglio. Terza, & Vltima parte.	13
Acerbe doglie. Prima parte.	14
Stillano. Seconda parte.	15
Donna Celeste. Prima parte.	15
Donna sublime. Seconda parte.	16
Donna ch'auuolgi. Terza parte.	17
Donna in cui. Quarta, & Vlt. parte.	18
La matutina aurora. Prima parte.	19
Sopra de gli arboscelli. Seconda parte.	20
Ecco che l'alba. Terza parte.	21
Ognun corra. Quarta, & Vlt. parte.	22
Ecco riede. Aria.	23
Pulchra es.	24
Veni sponsa Christi.	26
Regina Cęli.	27
Ego flos campi.	29
Salue, Latina.	30

A DOI VOCI.

Salue Regina volgare.	32
Dialogo. Giesù nel tuo partire.	33
Ecco che i monti indora. Prima parte.	35
O padre alto de i lumi. Seconda parte.	36
Al padre al figlio sia. Quarta, & VI. par.	36
Alta cosa è il mio Dio.	37

A TRE VOCI.

Ecco vien fuor la notte.	39
Occhi del Ciel ardenti. Prima parte.	40
Sian con i vostri lumi. Seconda parte.	41
Nel Ciel lucente. Terza, & Vlt. parte.	42
Alzate al sommo Ciel. Prima parte.	43
Sia benedetta. Seconda parte.	43
Sian benedetti. Quinta parte.	44
E voi genti. Sesta, & Vltima parte.	44
Torna la sera bruna. Prima parte.	46
Salua mè Signor. Seconda parte.	46
Mentre mi stai. Terza parte.	48
Fammi Signor. Quarta parte.	48
Sia laude. Quinta, & Vltima parte.	49
Litanie della Beata Vergine.	72

A QVATTRO VOCI.

Dio ti salui Maria.	50
Dialogo. O tù che vai per via.	52
O del gran Redentor.	54
Aue Maria speranza mia.	58
Io non saprei. Prima parte.	60
Il Ciel corona pose. Seconda parte.	62
Ella si reca. Terza parte.	64
Ella gl'agricoltori. Quarta parte.	66
E ver ch'in terra nasce. Quinta parte.	68
Il mondo dunque. Sesta, & Vlt. Parte.	70

IL FINE.

Plate 4. Giovanni Francesco Anerio, *Selva armonica* (Rome, 1617), *Tavola* from the Canto partbook. Courtesy of the Biblioteca del Conservatorio di Santa Cecilia, Rome.

Selva armonica

Dedication

Alla molto ill[ust]re sig[no]ra mia e padrona osser[vandissi]ma la sig[nora] Isabella Avila

La mia *Selva Armonica* non ho voluto sia vista dal mondo sotto altro nome, che di quello al cui intuito e richiesta in diversi tempi ho composto, in occasioni parimente diverse, che però diverse sono anco le opre che sono in essa. La richiesta fu di V[ostra] S[ignoria] mentre li davo lezione di musica, e questa mi spinse a punto a mandarla fuori fregiata del nome suo, per far conoscere nell'istesso tempo ed a lei ed alli signori suo padre e madre la memoria che tengo de' favori continui che ricevo da casa loro. M'assicuro che gradirà V[ostra] S[ignoria] il dono, come io ricevei volentieri il carico di dare alle stampe queste mie fatiche, quali accompagnarò al suo tempo con altre per aumentarli tuttavia maggiormente il desiderio di far maggior profitto nella musica, come ha fatto fin qui in età così tenera con tanto gusto e de' suoi genitori e mio insieme. E le bacio le mani. Di Roma il dì 10 agosto 1617.

Di V[ostra] S[ignoria] molto illustre affezionatissimo servitore
Gio[vanni] Francesco Anerio.

To the most illustrious lady, my patroness most worthy, Lady Isabella Avila.

I did not want my *Selva armonica* to be seen in the world under any other name than the one at whose intuition and request I composed it, on occasions as diverse as are the works contained in it. Your Ladyship requested it while I was giving you music lessons, and that request prompted me to issue this book, adorned with your name, to show at the same time to you and the Lords your father and mother, the memory I hold of the continual favors I receive from your house. I am sure that Your Ladyship will enjoy this gift, as I accepted with pleasure the charge of sending these works of mine to the press; I will add other works some other time to raise more and more your desire to progress in music, as you did up to now in your earliest years, pleasing your parents and me so much. And I kiss your hands. From Rome, the 10th of August, 1617.

The most devoted servant of Your most illustrious Ladyship
Giovanni Francesco Anerio.

Comment. The text has been treated according to the policies outlined in the "Texts and Translations." For original spellings and orthography, see plate 2.

1. Sommo Re delle stelle

Agostino Manni

Som- mo Re del- le stel- le, Qual gran pie--tà ti strin- - se, Qual a- mor ti so- spin- se A ve--nir giù dal cie- - lo, Pren- - der di car- ne il ve- - lo E suc-chiar le mam-mel- le De la be- a- ta Tua Ge- ni- tri- ce a- ma- - - ta? O vi- ta, o mio ri- sto- ro, O spe-

-me del mio cor, t'amo e t'adoro, T'adoro e benedico, T'adoro e benedico, In ni e lauditi dico, Unigenito Figlio, Che fai tremar col ciglio ogni superbo. Tu sei del Padre il Verbo E a la sua destra sedi E calchi il ciel, ⟨e calchi il ciel⟩ coi pie-

-di. A te mi volgo, riverente e prono, riverente e prono: Ti dimando perdono, Ti dimando perdono E del tuo amor stupendo Grazie eterne ti rendo, E del tuo amor stupendo Grazie eterne ti rendo, Grazie eterne ti rendo.

2. Dal tuo volto beato

Dal tuo vol- to be- a- to E- sco- no fol- go- ran- do, Ge- sù, per o- gni la- to Mil- le fiam- me d'a- mor, mil- le fiam- me d'a- mor, che sfa- vil- lan- do A- vam- pa- no il mio co- re, A- vam- pa- no il mio co- re, On- de e- gli ar- de e non mo- re,

25
On- de e- gli ar- de e non mo- - re.

30 *Seconda parte*
Ar- de il co- re e non mo- - re, Per- ché di co- tal fiam- ma

36
Quan- to più e più s'in- fiam- ma, Tan- to più si rav- vi- va: o dol- ce ar-

41
-do- re, Tan- to più si rav- vi- va: o dol- ce ar- do- re,

47
Non sia mai di te pri- vo, Ch'al-tra- men- te, ⟨ch'al-tra-men-

52
-te⟩ non vi- vo, Ch'al-tra- men- te, ⟨ch'al- tra- men- te⟩ non vi- vo.

Terza parte

Al- tra- men- te non vi- vo, An- zi mor- to sa- re- -i E se d'al- tro a- mor vi- vo, Fi- ni- scan to- sto i bre- vi gior- ni mie- i, Fi- ni- scan to- sto i bre- vi gior- ni mie- i, Né mi ri- scal- din ma- i I tuoi co- cen- - - - ti ra- i, I tuoi co- cen- - - - ti ra- i.

Quarta ed ultima parte

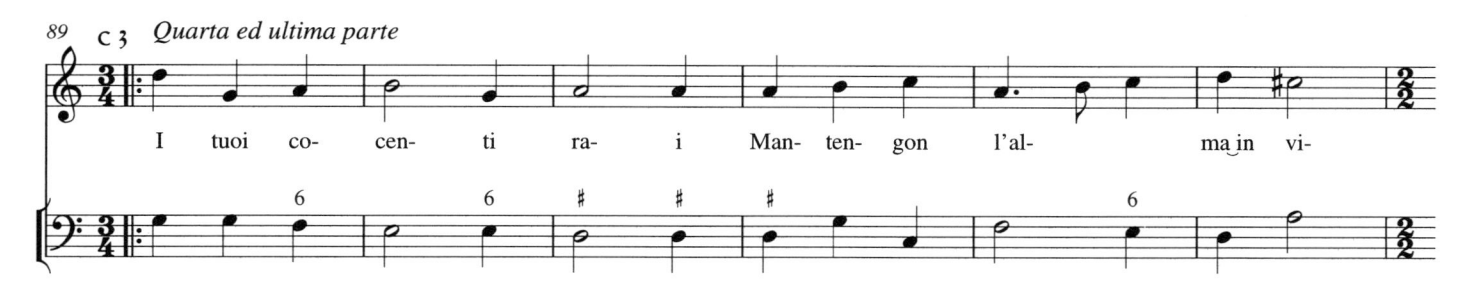

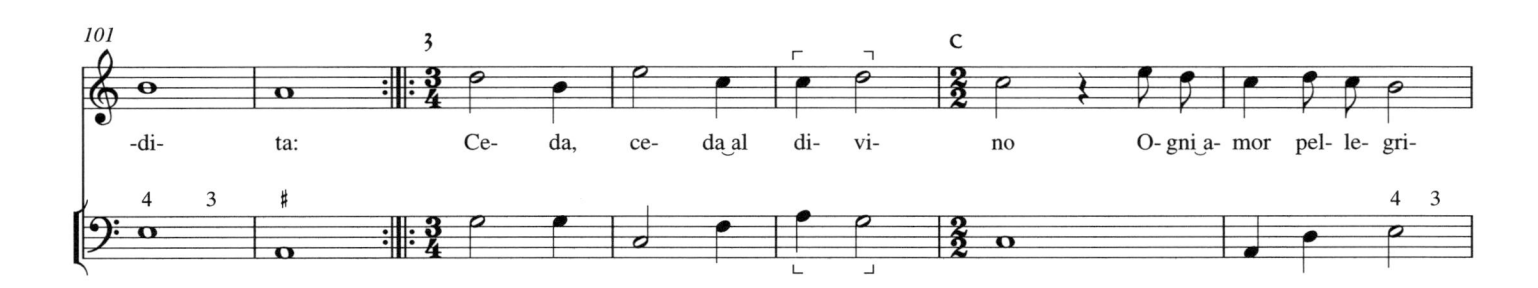

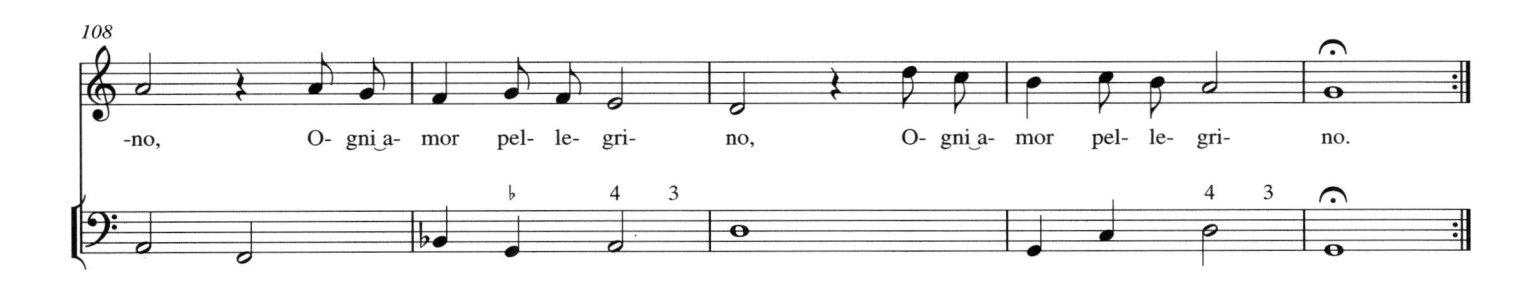

I tuoi cocenti rai Mantengon l'alma in vita, Né luce altra già mai Al mio cor sia gioconda, né gradita: Ceda, ceda al divino Ogni amor pellegrino, Ogni amor pellegrino, Ogni amor pellegrino.

3. Il tempo passa e mai più si ritrova

Aria in ottava rima

Il tempo passa e mai più si ritrova
E quel ch'ha da venir l'istesso pate;
Di mortal cosa non si può dar nuova,
Che dal tempo vien tolta in ogni etate.
Il tempo in ogni tempo il tutto acova
D'inverno, autunno, primavera, e state:
O van de-

11

-sio, pu- ro di- scor- so u- ma- no, Quan- to sei in-gor- do, i- nav- ver-

-ti- to e in- sa- no!

Seconda parte
Pas- sa- no i gior- ni e gli van die- tro gli an- ni,

Scor- ron l'e- ta- di e ci man-

-ca la vi- ta, Non ci la- scian di lor al- tro ch'af-

-fan- ni. Ri- tar- di in lun- go pur la sua par- ti- ta:

62
Pu- ro di- scor- so u- man, quan- to t'in- gan- ni A por le tue spe-
67
-ran- ze in chi te svi- - ta! Ri- tor- na in
72
te, ri- ti- ra- ti in di- spar- - te E vol- gi gli oc- chi ov'hai sì
77
de- gna par- - - te.
82
Terza ed ultima parte
Di gior- no in gior- no no- stra vi- ta a ba- - da La
88
mor- te tie- - ne e ci vien spes- so ap- pres- so E per-

-ché te- me o- gnun del- la sua spa- da El- la s'a- scon- de e ci ap- pre- sen- ta un mes- so: Il suo ve- ni- re, il quan- do e per qual stra- da Noi non sap- pia- mo e siam cru- cia- ti spes- so, Se- gno che tut- to il mon- do in un de- si- o Pas- sa, ec- cet- to ch'a- mar l'e- ter- no Di- o.

4. O dolce amor, Gesù

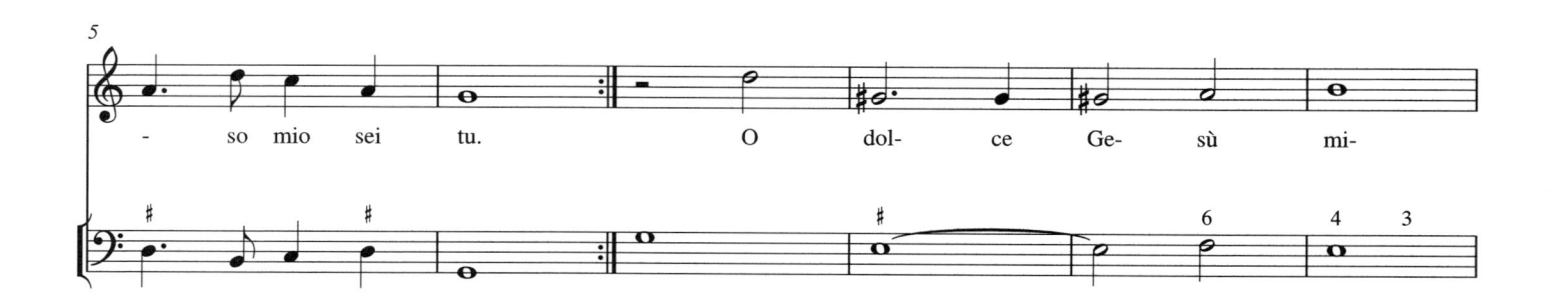

O dol- ce a- mor, Ge- sù, Lo spo- so mio sei tu. O dol- ce Gesù mi- o, La spo- sa tua son i- o.

Or fam- mi gra- zia, ch'em- pia tuo de- si- o E non t'of- fen- da, e non t'of- fen- da, e non t'of-

26
-fen- - - - da più.
31 Seconda parte
Tu bian- co più che gi- glio, Più di ro- sa ver- mi- glio, Più di ro- sa ver-
36
-mi- glio, Il ca- po hai tut- to d'o- ro. Se non ti ve-
41
- do io mo- - - - ro
46
E se ti ve- do in cro- ce ho gran mar- to- - -
52
-ro: Chi mi da- rà con- si- - - glio?

58
Chi mi da- rà con- si- — — glio?

63 *Terza ed ultima parte*
Me- glio è per te mo- ri- re, ⟨Me- glio è per te mo-

69
-ri- re,⟩ Che per al- tri gio- i- re, ⟨Che per al- tri

74
go- i- re.⟩ Me- glio è per te mo- ri- re, Che in

80
al- tri de- li- zia- — — re.

85
Dam- mi, Ge- sù, dam- mi, Ge- sù, per gra- zia sin- go- la-

17

5. Acerbe doglie e voi, piaghe amorose

31
d'a- pe fra purpureee ro- - - se.
37
Seconda parte
Stil- la- no gli occhi la- gri- me pie- to- se, Men-
44
- tre ch'ad u- na ad u- na vi re- mi- - ro E di- co "Ohi-
51
-mè, ohi- mè,— con un dol- - ce so- spi- ro— Co- me fu- - ste al mio
58
Dio a- spre e pe- no- - se, Co- me fu- - ste al mio
65
Dio a- spre e pe- no- - se, a- spre e pe- no- se!"

6. Donna celeste, che di Dio sei Madre

Canzonetta

Prima parte

Don- na ce- le- ste, che di Dio sei Ma- dre, Og- gi al tuo par- to, og- gi al tuo par- to scen- - - don mil- le squa- dre D'an- gio- li san- ti Con dol- ci can- ti, D'an- gio- li san- ti Con dol- ci can- ti: Ma- ri- a, fe- - li- - ce te!

31
Seconda parte
Don- na su- bli- me, ⟨don- na su- bli- me,⟩ ch'hai por- ta-
36
-to in ter- ra La ve- ra pa- - ce, la ve- ra
41
pa- - - ce, a noi tol- - ta hai
46
la guer- ra. Sa- tan s'a- di- ra, Sa- tan s'a- di-
51
-ra, Il ciel s'a- mi- ra, Il ciel s'a- mi-
57
-ra: Gio- i- - -

-sca il mon- do in te, Gio- i-

-sca il mon- do in te!

Terza parte

Don- na, ch'av- vol- gi den- tro al- le tue brac- cia Co- lui che tut- to l'u- ni- ver- so ab- brac- cia, Fat- to bam- bi- no E pic- co- li- no, Fat- to bam- bi- no E pic- co-

91
C
-li- no, Lo strin- - - - gi for-
96
- te a te, Lo strin- - - gi for- te a te.
4 3
5 6 4 3
102
Quarta ed ultima parte
Don- na, in cui so- -
107
- no tai bel- lez- - ze spar- -
111
- - - - se, Che 'l
5 6
115
Ver- bo e- ter- no ri- sguar- dot- - ti ed ar- se, Che 'l Ver- bo e- ter- no
5 6

ri- sguar- dot- - ti ed ar- se; O- ra ri- den-
-do, O- ra ri- den- - do Ti stai, _____ go- den-
-do, O- ra ri- den- - do Ti stai, _____
_____ go- den- do: Fe- li- - ce, dun- que,
te, Fe- li- - ce, fe- li- - ce, _____
_____ dun- - que, te!

7. La matutina aurora

Canzonetta

Prima parte

La ma- tu- ti- na au- ro- ra Già d'o- gni in- tor- no in- do- ra E fa mor- mo- rar l'on- de E tre- mo- lar le fron- de, E tre- mo- lar le fron- de.

Seconda parte

So- pra de gli ar- bo- scel- li Fa che i vez- zo- si au- gel- li Can- tin so- a- ve- men- te E ri-

da l'o- rï- en- te, E ri- da l'o- rï- en- te.

Terza parte

Ec- co, ec- co che l'al- ba ap- pa- re E si spec- chia nel ma- re -re E ras- se- re- -ma il cie- lo Già co- -per- to di ge-

27

-lo, Già coper- - - -to di ge- lo. E ras-se- -lo.

[Dal segno]

Quarta ed ultima parte

O-gnun cor- ra a ve- der- la, O-gnun cor- ra a ve- der- la, Ch'o- gni cam-pa- gna im- -per- la, Ch'o- gni cam-pa-gna im- per- - - la

E col sof- fiar de- l'au- -ra O-gni ar- so cor ri- stau- ra, O-gni ar- so cor, ⟨o-gni ar- so cor, o-gni ar- so cor⟩ ri- stau- - - ra.

8. Ecco riede, ecco soggiorna
Aria

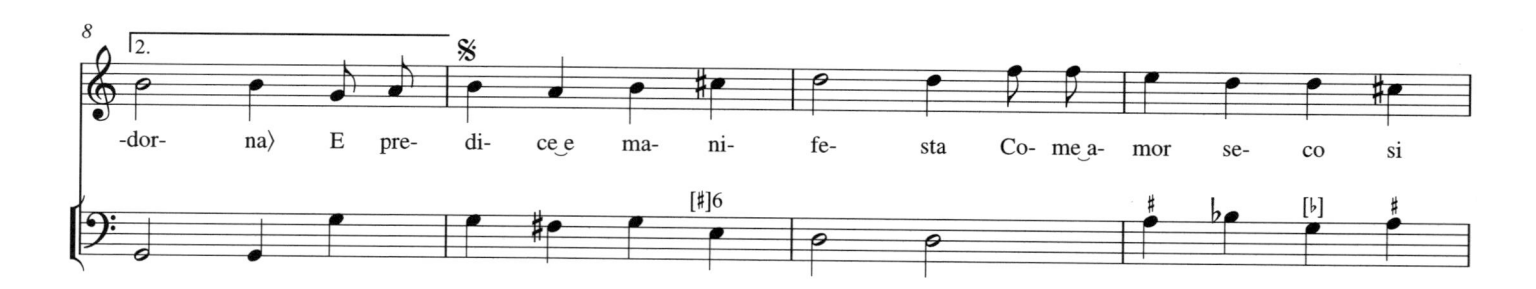

2. Ecco scaccia il verno e toglie
   Primavera le sue voglie
   E le più ruzzute piante
   Tornan vive al suo sembiante.

3. Ecco i prati e gli arboscelli
   Verdeggianti si fan belli
   E di coloriti fiori
   Primavera dà gli odori.

4. Ecco i monti alpestri e i mari,
   Tutti ombrosi e d'acque chiari,
   E gli augelli in mille modi
   Danno a primavera lodi.

9. Pulchra es

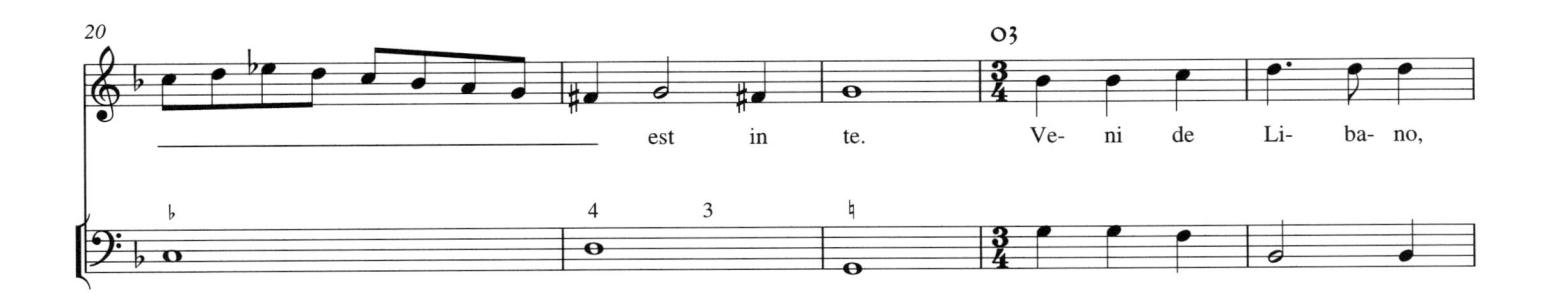

⟨ve- ni de Li- ba- no,⟩ spe- ci- o- sa me- a,
ve- ni de Li- ba- no, spe- ci- o- sa me- -
C
- - a, ve- ni, ve- ni, co-
- - - - ro- na-
- be- ris, ve- ni, ve- ni, co-
- - - -

- ro- na- be- ris; de ca- pi- te A- man,

de cu- bi- li- bus le- o- num, de cu- bi- li- bus le-

-o- num, de mon- ti- bus, ⟨de mon- ti- bus⟩ par- do-

-rum, de mon- ti- bus, ⟨de mon- ti- bus⟩ par- do- -

-rum. Vul- ne- ra- sti, ⟨vul- ne-

-ra- sti⟩ cor me- um, vul- ne- ra- sti,

⟨vul- ne- ra- sti⟩ cor me- -um in u- no o- cu- lo- rum tu- -o- -rum, et in u- no cri- ne col- li tu- i. Quam pul- chrae sunt mam- mae tu- ae, Quam pul- chrae sunt mam- mae tu- ae! Pul- chri- o- ra sunt u- -be- ra tu- a vi- no, pul- chri- o- ra sunt u- -be- ra tu- a vi- no, et o- dor un- guen- to- -rum tu- o- -rum su- per om- ni- -a a- ro- ma- ta, et o- dor un- guen- to- -rum tu- o- -rum su- per om- ni- a a- -ro- -ma- ta.

10. Veni sponsa Christi

-nam, quam ti- bi Do- -mi- nus, quam ti- bi Do- -mi- nus prae- pa- -ra- vit in ae- ter- - nam, prae- pa- -ra- vit in ae- ter- - - nam, prae- pa- ra- vit in ae- ter- - - - nam.

11. Regina caeli

37

12. Ego flos campi

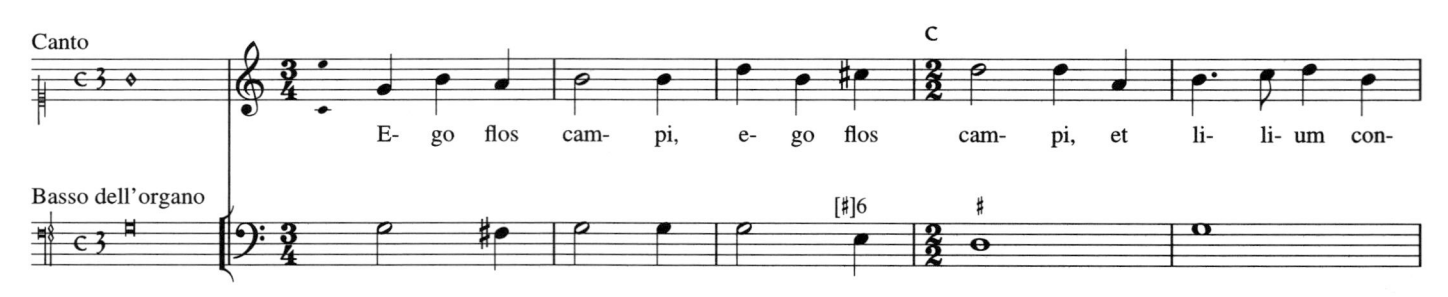

12
li- li- um in- ter spi- - nas, sic a- mi- - ca me-
17
-a in- - ter fi- - li- as.
23
Sic- ut ma- lum in- ter li- gna sil- va- -
28
- - rum, sic di- le- ctus me-
34
-us in- - - ter fi- - li- os.
40
Sub um- bra il- li- us, ⟨sub um- bra il- li-

-us) quem de- si- de- ra- ve- ram se- di, et fru- ctus e- ius dul- cis gut- tu- ri me- o, et fru- ctus e- ius dul- cis gut- tu- ri me- o, dul- cis, dul- cis gut- tu- ri me- o.

13. Salve, Regina

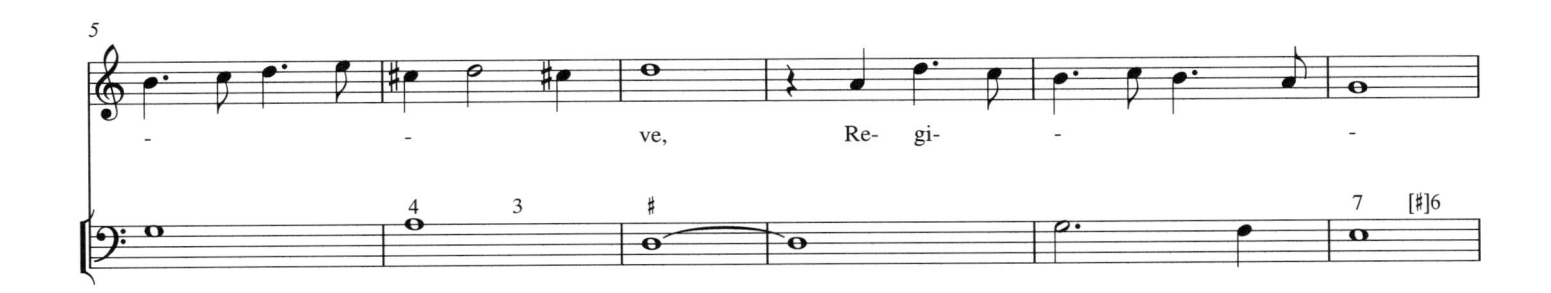

Sal- - - - - ve, Re- gi- - - na, ma- ter mi- se- - - ri- cor- di- ae: vi- ta, dul- ce- do, et spes no-

-stra, sal- ve. Ad te cla- ma- mus, ⟨ad te cla- ma-
-mus,⟩ ex- su- les fi- li- i He- - vae.
Ad te su- spi- ra-
-mus, ge- men- tes et flen- tes in hac
la- cri- ma- rum val- - - le.
E- ia er- go, ⟨e- ia er- go,⟩ Ad- vo- ca-

-ta nostra, illos tuos misericordes oculos ad nos converte. Et Jesum, benedictum fructum ventris tui, nobis post hoc exsilium, nobis post hoc exsilium osten-

86
-de. O cle- - mens:
91
pi- - a: o dul- cis Vir-
96
-go Ma- - - -
100
- - ri- a, o dul- cis Vir-
105
-go Ma- - - -
109
- ri- a, Vir- go Ma- ri- a.

14. Salve Regina, Madre divina

Agostino Manni

*Basso optional. See the critical notes.

46

47

O mia avvocata Santa e beata,

Quegli occhi tuoi Santi, se vuoi, Per la tua fé Rivolgi a me

E dopo questa Stanza molesta Del

63
tuo bel Fi- glio Bian- - co͜ e ver- - mi-
tuo bel Fi- glio Bian- - co͜ e ver-
68
- glio Nel pa- ra- di- so Mo- - stra- mi͜ il vi-
-mi- glio Nel pa- ra- di- so Mo- - stra- mi͜ il vi-
73
- so, Nel pa- ra- di- so Mo- stra-mi͜ il vi-
- so, Nel pa- ra- di- so Mo- stra-mi͜ il vi- -
79
- so, Mo- stra-mi͜ il vi- - - so.
- so, Mo- stra-mi͜ il vi- - so.

15. Gesù, nel tuo partire

Dialogo a 2

Anima, Cristo

*Or tenore. See the critical notes.

Anima: Del tuo sublime onore Gioisco, almo Signore, Ma come voi ch'io viva, Se di te, amor, son priva?

Cristo: Meco sempre star puoi, Anima, se tu vuoi.

Anima: Questo pur mi consola, Se ben rimango r sola; Ma 'l mondo non intende

co- me sia Che par- ten- do tu, dol- ce vi- ta mi- a, Io te- co sem- - - pre sti- a.

Cristo: Nel- la mia bel- la j- ma- - go L'oc- chio di mi- rar va- -go Pren- de- rà tal di- let- to Qual non ca- - pe in- tel- -let- to.

Anima: Ma quan- do fia quel ___

80
giorno Ch'io miri il viso adorno? Spo- so di-
Spo- so di-
6 4 3
86
-let- to e ca- ro, A me par trop- po a- ma- - ro
-let- to e ca- ro, A me par trop- po a- ma- ro
6 6 6 6 5 4 3 ♯
91
Man- car del- la tua vi- sta, La cui for- za con- qui- sta
Man- car del- la tua vi- sta, La cui for- za con- qui- sta
♯ ♯
96
O- gni ru- bel- lo co- re: Pur da me fug- gi, fug- gi, a-mo-
O- gni ru- bel- lo co- re: Pur da me fug- gi, fug- gi, a- mo- re,
6 4 3 ♯ ♯

fug- gi, fug- gi, a- mo- - - re, Pur da me fug- gi, fug- gi, a-
fug- gi, fug- gi, a- mo- - re, Pur da me fug- gi, fug- gi, a-

fug- gi, fug- gi, a- mo- re, fug- gi, fug- gi, a- mo- - re!
-mo- re, fug- gi, fug- gi, a- mo- - - re!

16. Ecco che i monti indora

Agostino Manni

-di- ta Lu- ce, che dà la vi- ta, Mi- ra la sua bel- lez- za,

-di- ta Lu- ce, che dà la vi- ta, Mi- ra la sua bel-

Mi- ra la sua bel- lez- za E o- gni al- tra co- sa sprez-

-lez- za E o- gni al- tra co- sa sprez-

-za, E o- gni al- tra co- sa sprez- za.

-za, E o- gni al- tra co- sa sprez- za.

Seconda parte

C1: O Pa- dre al- to dei lu- mi, Sian pu- ri i

B. org.

miei co- stu- - mi E ac- cen- di nel mio
co- re La fiam-ma del-l'a- mo- - - -
- re, E ac- cen- di nel mio co- re La fiam-ma del- l'a- mo-
- - - - re.
Terza parte
C2
B. org.
Fam- mi ve- der ch'è va- na O- gni gran- dez- za u- ma- na, O- - gni gran-dez-
- za u- ma- - - na E che 'l tem- po che

passa Tutte l'altezze abbassa, E che 'l tempo che passa, ⟨E che 'l tempo che passa⟩ Tutte l'altezze abbassa, Tutte l'altezze abbassa.

03 *Quarta ed ultima parte*

C1: Al Padre [e] al Figlio sia Imperio e signoria,

C2: Al Padre e al Figlio sia Imperio e signoria,

B. org.

101
Ed al di- vin A- mo- re Sia sem- pi- ter- no o-
Ed al di- vin A- mo- re Sia sem- pi- ter- no o- no- re,
107
-no- re, Sia sem- pi- ter- no o- no- - re,
Sia sem- pi- ter- no o- no- - - re,
[♯]
4 3
113
Ed al di- vin A- mo- re Sia sem- pi- ter- no o-
Ed al di- vin A- mo- re Sia sem- pi- ter- no o- no- re,
119
-no- re, Sia sem- pi- ter- no o- no- - re.
Sia sem- pi- ter- no o- no- - - re.
4 3

17. Alta cosa è il mio Dio

Agostino Manni

gran Signor delle virtù mirande! Ma non è buono il
mio Signore, Se non a gente che ha retto il cuore.
Udite, o cieli, Levate i veli E a noi mostrate La Deitate!

Ma ____ non si può mirar tanto splendore, Se non luce nel cor luce d'amore. Sta con noi chi fé noi, né se n'avvede Il cuor che non ha fede. O maraviglia eterna! La Maiestà su-

C
-per- na Di star- si sem- pre‿ha sta- bi- li- to‿il pat- to Con le co- se cre-
-a- - te che‿el- la‿ha fat- to. Il mio
Il mio
Dio sta na- sco- sto E 'l luo- co suo den- - tro‿a le co- se‿ha
Dio sta na- sco- sto E 'l luo- co suo den- - tro‿a le co- se‿ha
po- sto. Sta‿il mio Si- gnor se- cre- to
po- sto. Sta‿il mio Si- gnor se- cre- to

E nei riposi suoi giace quieto

E nei riposi suoi giace quieto

E, mentre stassi agli occhi nostri ignoto,

E, mentre stassi agli occhi nostri ignoto,

Dona a le cose sue la vita e 'l moto.

Dona a le cose sue la vita e 'l moto.

O cuori, udite, Cuori, stupite, O cuori, udite,

O cuori, udite, Cuori, stupite, O cuori, udite,

Cuori, stupite: Il Signor che è con meco e con esso io è sommo, eterno e incomprensibil Dio, Il Signor che è con meco, il Signor che è con meco e con esso io è sommo, eterno e incomprensibil Dio.

18. Ecco vien fuor la notte

Agostino Manni

Ecco vien fuor la notte Da le profonde grotte: Voi, del ciel Luce eterna, Siate al mio cor lucerna, Acciò ch'in mezzo al l'ombre Notturne non m'in-

-gom-bre Di te- ne- bre il pen- sie- ro, non m'in-gom-bre Di te- ne- bre il pen- sie-

non m'in-gom- bre Di te- ne- bre il pen- sie- -

non m'in-gom- bre Di te- ne- bre il pen- sie- -

-ro Il mio ne- mi- co fie- ro, Il mio ne- mi- co fie-

-ro Il mio ne- mi- co fie- ro, Il mio ne- mi- co fie- -

-ro Il mio ne- mi- co fie- ro, Il mio ne- mi- co fie-

-ro. Ve- ni- - te, al- to Si- gno- re, In guar- dia del mio

-ro. Ve- ni- - te, al- to Si- gno- re, In guar- dia del mio

-ro. Ve- ni- te, al- to Si- gno- re, In guar- dia del mio

co- re, Per- ché non sia gra- va- to Dal son- no
co- re, Per- ché non sia gra- va- to Dal son- no del pec- ca-
co- re, Per- ché non sia gra- va- to Dal son- no del pec-

del pec- ca- to, Ché, dop- po il mio ri- po- so, Nel
- to, Ché, dop- po il mio ri- po- so, Nel
-ca- to, Ché, dop- po il mio ri- po- so, Nel

gior- no lu- mi- no- so Di- rò con lie- to co- re Un in- no in vo-
gior- no lu- mi- no- so Di- rò con lie- to co- re Un in- no in vo- stro o-
gior- no lu- mi- no- so Di- rò con lie- to co- re

-stro o- no- re, Ché, dop- po il mio ri- po- so, Nel gior- no lu- mi-

-no- re, Ché, dop- po il mio ri- po- so, Nel gior- no lu- mi-

Ché, dop- po il mio ri- po- so, Nel gior- no lu- mi-

-no- so Di- rò con lie- to co- re Un in- no in vo- stro o- no-

-no- so Di- rò con lie- to co- re Un in- no in vo- stro o- no-

-no- so Di- rò con lie- to co- re Un

-re, Un in- no in vo- stro o- no- re.

-re, Un in- no in vo- stro o- no- re, in vo- stro o- no- re.

in- no in vo- stro o- no- re.

19. Occhi del cielo ardenti

15
-ne E so- pra il pro- prio man- to Ar- de- te al- tie- re tan-
-ne E so- - pra il pro- prio man- to Ar- de- te al- tie- re tan-
-ne E so- pra il pro- prio man- to Ar- de- te al- tie- re tan-
6
4 3
20
-to Al- la ve- nu- ta ch'o- ra Fa nel mon- do l'au- ro- ra, Fa nel
-to Al- la ve- nu- ta ch'o- ra Fa nel mon- do l'au-
-to Al- la ve- nu- ta ch'o- ra Fa nel mon- do l'au- ro-
♯ 7 6 ♯ ♮
25
mon- do l'au- ro- ra, Fa nel mon- do l'au- ro- ra, Fa nel mon- do l'au-
-ro- ra, Fa nel mon- do l'au- ro- ra, Fa nel mon- do l'au-
-ra, Fa nel mon- do l'au- ro- ra, Fa nel mon- do l'au-
5 6 6 5 6 5

29
C 3 Seconda parte
-ro- ra. Sian con i vo- stri lu- mi Sco- per- ti i
-ro- ra. Sian con i vo- stri lu- mi Sco- per- ti i
-ro- ra. Sian con i vo- stri lu- mi Sco- per- ti i
35
C
suoi co- stu- mi: Ch'a l'un e l'al- tro po- lo
suoi co- stu- mi: Ch'a l'un e l'al- tro po- lo
suoi co- stu- mi: Ch'a l'un e l'al- tro po- lo
40
El- la si sten- de a vo- lo E
El- la si sten- de a vo- lo E se- co coi bei
E se- co

se- co coi bei rag- - gi Il sol fa
rag- - gi Il
coi bei rag- - gi Il sol fa
— i suoi viag- gi, fa i suoi viag- gi, Per ri- por- tar vit- to- ri-
sol fa i suoi viag- gi, Per ri- por- tar vit- to- ri-
i suoi viag- gi, Per ri- por- tar vit- to- ri-
-a Di sua do- vu- ta glo- ri- a, Di sua do- vu- ta glo-
-a Di sua do- vu- ta glo- ri- a, Di sua do-
-a Di sua do- vu- ta glo- ri- a, Di sua do- vu- ta

-ria, Di sua do- vu- ta glo- ri- a.
-vu- ta glo- ri- a, Di sua do- vu- ta glo- ri- a.
glo- ri- a, Di sua do- vu- ta glo- ri- a.

Terza ed ultima parte

Nel ciel lu- cen- ti, nel ciel lu-
Nel ciel lu- cen- ti, nel ciel lu- cen-
Nel ciel lu- cen- ti, nel ciel lu- cen-

-cen- ti stel- le, Fa- te- vi tut- te bel- le, Quan- do l'al- ba ce-
- ti stel- le, Fa- te- vi tut- te bel- le, Quan- do l'al- ba ce-
- ti stel- le, Fa- te- vi tut- te bel- le, Quan- do l'al- ba ce-

73
-le- ste Il re- al man- to ve- ste, Ac- ciò che d'o- gni in- tor- no Si
-le- ste Il re- al man- to ve- ste, Ac- ciò che d'o- gni in- tor- no Si
-le- ste Il re- al man- to ve- ste, Ac- ciò che d'o- gni in- tor- no Si
♮ ♯ ♯
78
ve- da chia- ro il gior- no Al suo ve- nir cor- te- se, Al
ve- da chia- ro il gior- no E ren- da o- gni pa- e- se Al suo ve- nir cor-
ve- da chia- ro il gior- no E ren- da o- gni pa- e- se Al suo ve- nir cor-
6 6 ♯ ♮ 6 6 6 7 [♮]6 6
83
suo ve- nir cor- te- se, Al suo ve- nir, al suo ve- nir, al
-te- se, Al suo ve- nir cor- te- se, Al suo ve- nir cor- te- se, Al
-te- se, Al suo ve- nir cor- te- se, Al suo ve- nir cor-
4 3 5 6 4 3 4 3 9 6

88
suo ve- nir cor- te- - se, E ren- da o- gni pa-
suo ve- nir cor- te- - se, Al
-te- se, cor- te- - se, E ren- da o- gni pa-
5 6 4 3 6 6 6
93
-e- se Al suo ve- nir cor- te- se, Al suo ve- nir cor- te- se, ⟨Al
suo ve- nir cor- te- se, Al suo ve- nir cor- te- se, Al suo ve- nir, al
-e- se Al suo ve- nir cor- te- se, Al suo ve- nir cor-
7 [♮]6 6 4 3 5 6 4 3
98
suo ve- nir cor- te- se,⟩ Al suo ve- nir cor- te- - se.
suo ve- nir, al suo ve- nir cor- te- - se.
-te- se, Al suo ve- nir cor- te- se, cor- te- - se.
4 3 9 6 5 6 4 3

20. Alzate al sommo ciel memoria e mente

Agostino Manni

ciel ___ lu- cen- te, E 'l fab- - bro del- le stel- le lu- mi-

-tis- si- mo Re del ciel lu- cen- te, E 'l fab- - bro del- le stel- le lu- mi-

del ciel lu- cen- te, E 'l fab- - bro del- le stel- le lu- mi-

-no- se, Che fé tut- te le co- se, be- ne- di- te.

-no- se, Che fé tut- te le co- se, be- ne- di- te.

-no- se, Che fé tut- te le co- se, be- ne- di- te.

Seconda parte

C1: Sia be- ne- det- ta La Tri- ni- tà per- fet- ta, Che so- pra i cie- li sta Con

B. org.

glo- ria e ma- ie- stà E glo- ri- o- sa e de- gna Vi- ve be- a- ta e re - - - gna.

Terza parte

Sia benedetto il Padre Da le celesti squa-dre, Sia il Figlio benedetto Dal suo popolo eletto E il santo Spirto benedetto sia, Che col Padre e col Figlio ha si - gnoria.

Quarta parte

Sia benedetta ancora Maria, splendor del ciel, candida au-

Quinta parte

-ro- -ra, Che sot- to il pie- de tien la lu- -na au- ra- ta, Di stel- -le in co- -ro- na- ta.

Sian be- ne- det- ti Gli an- ge- li e- let- ti Con in- ni e can- ti;
Sian be- ne- det- ti Gli an- ge- li e- let- ti Con in- ni e can- ti;

Sian be- ne- det- ti i san- ti. E voi, Re del- le gen- ti, E
Sian be- ne- det- ti i san- ti. E voi, Re del- le gen- ti, E

voi, Regina mia, Con gli angeli lucenti, Coi santi in compagnia Benedite dal ciel la mente e 'l core Che benedice in terra il mio Signore, Che benedice in terra il mio Signore.

81

Sesta ed ultima parte

E voi, genti disperse, genti disperse Dove sorgono i monti e giran l'onde, Al ciel converse, Liete e gioconde, Come lau-

-do i- o, Be- ne- di- te l'al- tis- si- mo Re mi- o, Be- ne-
-do i- o, Be- ne- di- te l'al- tis- si- mo Re mi- o, Be- ne-
-do i- o, Be- ne- di- te l'al- tis- si- mo Re mi- o, Be- ne-

-di- te l'al- tis- si- mo Re mi- o. In- no gio- con- do
-di- te l'al- tis- si- mo Re mi- o.
-di- te l'al- tis- si- mo Re mi- o.

Si- a al Re del mon- do, In- no con can- to Ce- le- ste e
In- no con can- to Ce- le- ste e
In- no con can- to Ce- le- ste e

santo, In- no con can- to Ce- le- ste e san- to, Can- to con
santo, In- no con can- to Ce- le- ste e san- to, Can- to con
santo, In- no con can- to Ce- le- ste e san- to, Can- to con

sal- mi, can- to con sal- mi, sal- mi e lau- di e- ter- ne, Con vo- ci al-
sal- mi, can- to con sal- mi, sal- mi e lau- di e- ter- ne, Con
sal- mi, can- to con sal- mi, sal- mi e lau- di e- ter- ne,

-ter- ne, Con vo- ci al- ter- ne, Con ter- se
vo- ci al- ter- ne, al- ter- ne, Con ter- se no- te e con so- nan- te, con ter- se
Con vo- ci al- ter- ne, Con ter- se no- te e con so- nan- te

166
no- te con so- nan- - te ver- so Di- ca o- gni lin-
no- te con so- nan- te ver- so Di- ca o- gni lin-
ver- - so Di- ca o- gni lin-
4 3 ♯
171
-gua al Re del- l'u- ni- ver- so, Di- ca o- gni lin- gua al Re del-
-gua al Re del- l'u- ni- ver- so, Di- ca o- gni lin- gua
-gua, ⟨di- ca o- gni lin- gua⟩ al Re del-
6 5 6 3 3 3
176
-l'u- ni- ver- so, al Re del- l'u- - ni- ver- so.
al Re del- l'u- ni- ver- so, al Re del- l'u- ni- ver- so.
-l'u- ni- ver- so, al Re del- l'u- ni- ver- - so.
6 5 4 3

21. Torna la sera bruna

Aria

Agostino Manni

Prima parte

Canto primo: Tor- na la se- ra bru- na E in ciel lu- -ce la lu- na, E in ciel lu- ce la lu- na,

Canto secondo: Tor- na la se- ra bru- na E in ciel lu- -ce la lu- na, E in ciel lu- ce la lu- na,

Basso or Baritono*: Tor- na la se- ra bru- na E in ciel lu- -ce la lu- na, E in ciel lu- ce la lu- na,

Basso dell'organo

Che 'l mor- tal e- gro in vi- ta Al son- - no del-

N.B. This piece is notated almost entirely in coloration. See the critical notes.

*An alternative Baritono part duplicates the Basso part, but sets the lowest notes an octave higher. Cue size notes show passages where the Baritono departs from the Basso. The Baritono's range is B♭–d'; the original clef is F3.

17
1.
2.
-la vi- ta, Al son- - no del- la vi- ta. -ta.
-la vi- ta, Al son- - no del- la vi- ta. -ta.
-la vi- ta, Al son- - no del- la vi- ta. -ta.
5 6
24
Seconda parte
Sal- va me, Si- gnor for- te, Dal son- no del-
Sal- va me, Si- gnor for- te, Dal son- no del-
Sal- va me, Si- gnor for- te, Dal son- no del-
6
29
-la mor- te, Dal son- no del- la mor- te
-la mor- te, Dal son- no del- la mor- te
-la mor- te, Dal son- no del- la mor- te
6

34

E stam- mi sem- pre in- tor- no, Sin- ché _____ ri- tor-

E stam- mi sem- pre in- tor- no, Sin- ché _____ ri- tor-

E stam- mi sem- pre in- tor- no, Sin- ché _____ ri- tor-

40

|1. |2.

-ni il gior- no, Sin- ché _____ ri- tor- ni il gior- no. -no.

-ni il gior- no, Sin- ché _____ ri- tor- ni il gior- no. -no.

-ni il gior- no, Sin- ché _____ ri- tor- ni il gior- no. -no.

47 **Terza parte**

Men- tre mi stai pre- sen- te Fug- ga via in- con-

Men- tre mi stai pre- sen- te Fug- ga via in- con-

Men- tre mi stai pre- sen- te Fug- ga via in- con-

52
-ti- nen- te, Fug- ga via͜ in- con- ti- nen- te
-ti- nen- te, Fug- ga via͜ in- con- ti- nen- te
-ti- nen- te, Fug- ga via͜ in- con- ti- nen- te
57
In- nan- zi͜ al tuo splen- do- re La te- - ne- bra͜ e
In- nan- zi͜ al tuo splen- do- re La te- - ne- bra͜ e
In- nan- zi͜ al tuo splen- - do- re La te- - ne- bra͜ e
63
l'or- ro- re, La te- - ne- bra͜ e l'or- ro- re. -re.
l'or- ro- re, La te- - ne- bra͜ e l'or- ro- re. -re.
l'or- ro- re, La te- - ne- bra͜ e l'or- ro- re. -re.
1.
2.

Quarta parte

Fam- mi, Si- gnor di- let- to, Dor- mir so- pra il tuo pet- to, Dor- mir so- pra il tuo pet- to

E not- te e gior- no sti a Con te la vi-

86
1.
2.
-ta mi- a, Con te la vi- ta mi- a. -a.
-ta mi- a, Con te la vi- ta mi- a. -a.
-ta mi- a, Con te la vi- ta mi- a. -a.
[5] 6 ♯ ♮ ♮ [♮]
93
Quinta ed ultima parte
Sia lau- de, glo- ria e can- to Al Pa- dre, al Fi- glio e al san- to
Sia lau- de, glo- ria e can- to Al Pa- dre, al Fi- glio e al san-
Sia lau- de, glo- ria e can- to Al Pa- dre, al Fi- glio e al san-
[♮] ♭ ♯ [♮] 6 6
99
Spir- to, Al Pa- dre, al Fi- glio e al san- to Spir- to,
-to Spir- to, Al Pa- dre, al Fi- glio e al san- to Spir- to,
-to Spir- to, Al Pa- dre, al Fi- glio e al san- to Spir- to,
4 3 ♯ 6 ♭ ♯ ♯ [♮]

22. Dio ti salvi, Maria, Madre divina

Agostino Manni

6
De- gli‿an- ge- li Re- gi- na, De- gli‿an- ge- li Re- gi- na;
-dre di- vi- na, De- gli‿an- ge- li Re- gi- na, De- gli‿an- ge- li Re- gi- na;
De- gli‿an- ge- li Re- gi- na, De- gli‿an- ge- li Re- gi- na;
-dre di- vi- na, De- gli‿an- ge- li Re- gi- na, De- gli‿an- ge- li Re- gi- na;
12
Di lu- - - ce‿e glo-
Dio ti sal- vi, Ma- ria, stel- la se- re- na, Di lu- ce‿e glo- - ria
Dio ti sal- vi, Ma- ria, stel- la se- re- na,
Di lu- - ce‿e glo- - ria pie-
18
- ria pie- na, Di lu- ce‿e glo- - ria pie- na. Ver- gi- ne‿e-
pie- na, Di lu- - ce‿e glo- ria pie- na. Ver- gi- ne‿e-
Di lu- - ce‿e glo- - ria pie- na. Ver- gi- ne‿e-
- na. Ver- gi- ne‿e-

24
C
-ter- na, Ma- dre del- l'a- mo- re, Con te- co è il tuo Si- gno-
-ter- na, Ma- dre del- l'a- mo- re, Con te- co è il tuo Si- gno- re, Con te- co è il tuo Si- gno-
-ter- na, Ma- dre del- l'a- mo- re, Con te- co è il tuo Si- gno-
-ter- na, Ma- dre del- l'a- mo- re, Con te- co è il tuo Si- gno- -
31
3
C
-re. Be- ne- det- ta sii tu, Be- ne- det- ta sii tu E il tuo Fi- gliol dol-
-re. Be- ne- det- ta sii tu, Be- ne- det- ta sii tu E il tuo Fi- gliol dol-
-re. Be- ne- det- ta sii tu, Be- ne- det- ta sii tu E il tuo Fi- gliol dol-
-re. Be- ne- det- ta sii tu, Be- ne- det- ta sii tu E il tuo Fi- gliol dol-
39
-cis- si- mo Ge- sù. San- ta Ma- ri- a, Spe- ran-
-cis- si- mo Ge- sù. San- ta Ma-
-cis- si- mo Ge- sù.
-cis- si- mo Ge- sù.

Lyrics by voice:

Voice 1: -za mi- a, Spe- ran- za mi- a, San- ta Ma- ri- a, Spe- ran- za mi- a, Ma- dre di Di- o, Re- fu- gio mi- o,

Voice 2: -ri- a, Spe- ran- za mi- a, Spe- ran- za mi- a, San- ta Ma- ri- a, Spe- ran- za mi- a, Ma- dre di Di- o, Re- fu- gio mi- o,

Voice 3: San- ta Ma- ri- a, Spe- ran- za mi- a, San- ta Ma- ri- a, Spe- ran- za mi- a, Ma- dre di Di- o, Re- fu- gio mi- o,

Voice 4: San- ta Ma- ri- a, Spe- ran- za mi- a, Spe- ran- za mi- a, Ma- dre di Di- o, Re- fu- gio mi- o,

Prega il Signor per me, Prega per me, Signora, Or ch'ho bisogno e nella morte ancora. Così sia, così sia, Così sia, così sia, Dolce vergine Ma-

85
-ri- a, Co- sì si- a, co- sì si- a,
-ri- a, Co- sì si- a, co- sì si- a, Dol- ce ver- gi- ne Ma-
Co- sì si- a, co- sì si- a, Dol- ce ver- gi- ne Ma-
Co- sì si- a, co- sì si- a,
[♯]
[♯]6
93
Dol- ce ver- gi- ne Ma- ri- a, Dol- ce
-ri- a, Dol- ce ver- gi- ne Ma- ri- a,
-ri- a, Dol- ce ver- gi- ne Ma- ri- a,
Dol- ce ver- gi- ne Ma- ri- a, Dol- ce
100
ver- gi- ne Ma- ri- a, ⟨Dol- ce ver- gi- ne Ma- ri- a.⟩
Dol- ce ver- gi- ne Ma- ri- a.
Dol- ce ver- gi- ne Ma- ri- a.
ver- gi- ne Ma- ri- a, Dol- ce ver- gi- ne Ma- ri- a.

23. O tu, che vai per via

Dialogo a 4

Anima, Morte, Vita, Coro

21
-sio- ne. Nel- la ma- gio- ne Del cie- lo. La Ma-
Do- ve? E chi ci hai tu?
4 3 6
27
- dre di Ge- sù. Ho sol lo- da- to i
E per qual mer- to l'ha- i?
7 [#]6
33
Anima
ra- i Di sua ec- cel- len- za e po- i Ser- vi- to a i vo- ler
B. org.
[#]6 # # 6 5
38
suo- i. Ma tu, ch'o- gnor mi chia- mi, Al- tro da
4 3 [#]6 6 6 5
44
Anima
me più bra- mi? Il fin del- la mia
Morte
Il fin del- la tua vi- ta.
B. org.
6 # 6 4 3 6

vi- ta Ot- te- ner- lo non puo- i.

Ed a chi dar- la vuo-

A quel ch'è vi- ta e- ter- na Di glo- ria sem- pi- ter-

-i?

-na.

Non è com- mun e- dit- to, Ch'o- gnun da me sia af- flit-

-to?

Anima
Sì, ma non sem- pre a un mo- do.

Vita
Che sen- to, ve- do ed o- - do?

Morte

B. org.

Vita: Morte, non ha condegno Quest'alma del tuo regno E, perché Dio m'addita Ch'io venga a dargli vita, Meco esser gli consorte Sin a del ciel le porte.

Morte: Da poi che so' interdetta, Faccia quel fin ch'aspetta: Teco al celeste coro Vuo' recondurla.

Anima: Moro, moro!

(105) Coro
Canto
Alto
Tenore
Basso
B. org.
Vie- ni, a- ni- ma be- a- ta, Vie- ni, a- ni- ma be- a- ta, Co- lom-
Vie- ni, a- ni- ma be- a- ta, Vie- ni, a- ni- ma be- a- ta,
Vie- ni, a- ni- ma be- a- ta, Vie- ni, a- ni- ma be- a- ta,
Vie- ni, a- ni- ma be- a- ta, Vie- ni, a- ni- ma be- a- ta,
110
-bel- la d'a- mo- re, Vie- ni, a- ni- ma be- a- ta,
Co- lom- bel- la d'a- mo- re, Vie- ni, a- ni- ma be- a- ta,
Vie- ni, a- ni- ma be- a- ta, Co- lom-
Vie- ni, a- ni- ma be- a- ta,
114
Co- lom- bel- la d'a- mo- re,
Co- lom- bel- la d'a- mo- re,
-bel- la d'a- mo- re,
Co- lom- bel- la d'a- mo- re,

118
Vien, che sei e- sal- ta- ta Dal- l'e- ter- no Si- gno-
Vien, che sei e- sal- ta- ta Dal- l'e- ter- no Si- gno-
Vien, che sei e- sal- ta- ta Dal- l'e- ter- no Si- gno-
Vien, che sei e- sal- ta- ta Dal- l'e- ter- no Si- gno-
124
-re, Vien, che sei e- sal- ta- ta Dal- l'e- ter- no
-re, Vien, che sei e- sal- ta- ta Dal- l'e- ter- no
-re, Vien, che sei e- sal- ta- ta Dal- l'e- ter- no
-re, Vien, che sei e- sal- ta- ta Dal- l'e- ter- no
130
Si- gno- re, Dal- l'e- ter- no Si- gno- re.
Si- gno- re, Dal- l'e- ter- no Si- gno- re.
Si- gno- re, Dal- l'e- ter- no Si- gno- re.
Si- gno- re, Dal- l'e- ter- no Si- gno- re.

24. O del gran Redentor Madre alma e bella

Agostino Manni

16
Con la virtù di- vi- na Del- la tua man po- ten-
Con la virtù di- vi- na Del- la tua man po- ten-
Con la virtù di- vi- na Del- la tua man po- ten-
-la, Con la virtù di- vi- na
[♯] 6 6 ♯
21
-te Soc- cor- ri al- la ru- i- -
-te Soc- cor- ri al- la ru- i- na, Soc- cor- ri al- la ru- i-
-te Soc- cor- ri al- la ru- i- na, Soc-cor- ri al- la ru- i-
Soc- cor- ri al- la ru- i- na, Soc- cor- ri al- la ru- i-
♯ ♯ ♯ 9 8
26
- na Del- la smar- ri- ta gen- te, Che ca- -
-na Del- la smar- ri- ta gen- te,
-na Del- la smar- ri- ta gen- te,
-na Del- la smar- ri- ta gen- te, Che ca- -
♯ ♯ 4 3

31
- de, che ca- -
Che ca- - - de,
Che ca- - - de, che ca-
- de, che ca- -
35
- - de e mer- cé gri- - da E so- lo in
che ca- - de e mer- cé gri- da E so- lo in
- de, che ca- de e mer- - cé gri- - da E so- lo in
- - de e mer- cé gri- da E so- lo in
40
te, e so- lo in te si fi- - - da.
te, e so- lo in te si fi- - da.
te, e so- lo in te si fi- - da.
te, e so- lo in te si fi- - da.

45
C
Tu che, nel fior pri- mie- -
T
Tu che, nel fior, ⟨tu che, nel fior⟩ pri- mie- -
B. org.
52
-ro, Del sopran mes-sag- ge- ro Fe- li- ce udi- sti quel- la Dol- - ce sa- lu-
-ro, Del sopran mes-sag- ge- ro Fe- li- ce udi- sti quel- la Dol- - ce sa- lu- te, a-
58
-te, a- ma- ta ver- gi- nel- la, a- ma- ta ver- gi- nel-
-ma- ta ver- gi- nel- la, a- ma- ta ver- - gi- nel- -
63
C
-la, E più d'o- gni al- - tra pu- ra, Con stu- por di na-
A
E più d'o- gni al- - tra pu- ra, Con stu- por di na- tu- ra, di
T
-la, E più d'o- gni al- - tra pu- ra, Con stu- por di na- tu- ra, Con stu- por
B
E più d'o- gni al- - tra pu- ra, Con stu- por di na-
B. org.

-tu- ra, Ver- gi- ne in- nan- zi al sa- cro par- to e po-
-na- tu- ra, Ver- gi- ne in- nan- zi al sa- cro par- to e po-
-di na- tu- ra, Ver- gi- ne in- nan- zi al sa- cro par- to e po-
-tu- ra,

-i, Hai
-i, Ver- gi- ne in- nan- zi al sa- cro par- to e po- i,
-i, Ver- gi- ne in- nan- zi al sa- cro par- to e po- i,
Ver- gi- ne in- nan- zi al sa- cro par- to e po- i,

ge- ne- ra- to a no- i Il Ver- bo sem- pi- ter-

Si- gnor del ciel super-no, Abbracia i peccatori Coi tuoi beati amori

101
pec- ca- to- ri, Ab- brac- cia͜ i pec- ca- to- ri, ⟨Ab-
pec- ca- to- ri,⟩ Ab-
pec- ca- to- ri⟩ Coi tuoi be- a- ti͜ a- mo- ri, Ab- brac- cia͜ i pec- ca- to- - ri, ⟨Ab-
Coi tuoi be- a- ti͜ a- mo- - ri, Ab- brac- cia͜ i pec- ca- to- ri
♯ 6 5 4 3 6 7 6
106
-brac- cia͜ i pec- ca- to- ri⟩ Coi tuoi be- a- ti͜ a-
-brac- cia͜ i pec- ca- to- - ri Coi tuoi be- a- ti͜ a- mo-
-brac- cia͜ i pec- ca- to- ri⟩ Coi tuoi be- a- ti͜ a- mo- -
Coi tuoi be- a- ti͜ a- mo- ri,
4 3 6 5 [♯]6
110
-mo- ri, ⟨Coi tuoi be- a- ti͜ a- mo- ri.⟩
-ri, Coi tuoi be- a- ti, be- a- ti͜ a- mo- ri.
-ri, Coi tuoi be- a- ti͜ a- mo- ri, be- a- ti͜ a- mo- ri.
Coi tuoi be- a- ti͜ a- mo- ri, Coi tuoi be- a- ti͜ a- mo- ri.
6 5 4 3 [♯]

25. Ave Maria, Speranza mia

Agostino Manni

18
O te be- a- ta, Tra l'al- tre na- ta! Sia be- ne- det- to Il
⟨O te be- a- ta,⟩ Tra l'al- tre na- ta! Sia be- ne- det- to Il
O te be- a- ta, Tra l'al- tre na- ta!
⟨O te be- a- ta,⟩ Tra l'al- tre na- ta!
24
tuo di- let- to Ge- sù, mia vi- ta, Bon- tà in- fi- ni- ta.
tuo di- let- to Ge- sù, mia vi- ta, Bon- tà in- fi- ni- ta.
30
Ma- dre di Di- o, Con- for- to mi- o, Ma- dre di Di- o,
Ma- dre di Di- o, Con- for- to mi- o, Ma- dre di Di- o,
Ma- dre di Di- o, ⟨Ma- dre di Di- o,⟩
Ma- dre di Di- o, Ma- dre di Di- o,

36
Pre- ga il Si- gno- re Che per tuo a- mo- re
Pre- ga il Si- gno- re Che per tuo a- mo- re
Con- for- to mi- o, Pre- ga il Si- gno- re Che per tuo a- mo- re
Con- for- to mi- o, Pre- ga il Si- gno- re Che per tuo a- mo- re
42
A- prir mi fac- cia Con lie- ta fac- - cia,
A- prir mi fac- cia Con lie- ta fac- - cia,
A- prir mi fac- cia Con lie- ta
A- prir mi fac- cia Con lie- ta
6 5 4 3
48
C
Dop- - po la mor- - te,
Dop- - po la mor- - te,
fac- - cia, Dop- - po la mor- te, Del
fac- - cia, Dop- - po la mor- te,
6 5 4 3 4 3

113

26. Io non saprei dir quanto

Canzone sopra il canto della Cicala

14
-ca- la, la mia ca- ra, la mia ca- ra Ci- ca- la, la mia ca- - ra Ci- ca-
la mia ca- ra Ci- ca- la, Che man- - da fuor dal pet-
man- da fuor dal pet- to La mia ca- ra, la mia ca- ra Ci-
fuor dal pet- to La mia ca- ra Ci- ca- la,
5 6 6 6 5 6
19
-la, la mia ca- - ra Ci- ca- - la, le cui no- te
-to La mia ca- ra, ⟨la mia ca- ra⟩ Ci- ca- la, le cui no- te
-ca- la, la mia ca- - ra Ci- ca- la, le cui no- te
la mia ca- ra Ci- ca- - la, le cui no- te
5 6 ♯
24
Ci- gno o si- re- na pa- - reg- giar non po- te, Ci-
Ci- gno o si- re- na pa- - reg- giar non po- te, Ci-
Ci- gno o si- re- na pa- - reg- giar non po- te, Ci-
Ci- gno o si- re- na pa- - reg- giar non po- te, Ci-
♮ [♯]6 4 3

29
-gno o si- re- na pa- reg- giar non po- - te.
-gno o s.- re- na pa- reg- giar non po- te.
-gno o s.- re- na pa- reg- giar non po- te.
-gno o si- re- na pa- reg- giar non po- te.
6 4 3
34
Seconda parte
Il ciel co- ro- na po- se, Il ciel co-
Il ciel co- ro- na po- se, Il
Il ciel co- ro-
Il ciel co-
40
-ro- - na, co- ro- - na po- se
ciel co- ro- na po- se, co- ro- na po- se
- na po- se, co- ro- - na po- se
-ro- - na po- - se
6 6 5

Nella regal sua testa, Nella regal sua testa,
Nella regal sua testa,
Nella regal sua testa, Nella regal sua testa,
Nella regal sua testa, ⟨Nella regal sua testa,⟩

Non di caduche rose, Ma di rubin contesta,
Non di caduche rose, Ma di rubin contesta, contesta,
Non di caduche rose, Ma di rubin contesta,
Non di caduche rose, Ma di rubin contesta,

-sta,
-sta, Ond'a lei nel cantar com'a regi-
Ond'a lei nel cantar com'a regi-
-sta, Ond'a lei nel cantar com'a regi-

60
On- d'a lei nel ‿ can- tar co- - m'a re- gi-
-na, On- - d'a lei nel can- tar ‿ co- m'a re- gi-
-na, On- - d'a lei nel can- tar ‿ co- m'a re- gi-
-na
♯ 4 3
65
-na O- gni‿au- gel col ta- cer ce- de‿e s'in- - chi- na, ce- de‿e
-na O- gni‿au- gel col ta- cer ce- de‿e s'in- chi- na, ce- de‿e s'in-
-na O- gni‿au- gel ce- de‿e s'in-
O- gni‿au- gel col ta- cer ce- de‿e s'in- chi- na,
[♮] [♯] 5 9 8 4 3 [♮] 6 5
70
s'in- chi- na, O- gni‿au- gel col ta- cer, ⟨o- gni‿au- gel col ta-
- chi- na, O- gni‿au- gel col ta- cer, ⟨o- gni‿au- gel col ta-
-chi- na, O- gni‿au- gel col ta- cer, ⟨o- gni‿au- gel col ta-
O- gni‿au- gel col ta- cer, ⟨o- gni‿au- gel col ta-
9 ꞓ 4 3 6 [♮] [♮]

75
-cer〉 ce- de e s'in- chi- - na.
-cer〉 ce- de e s'in- - chi- na, ce- de e s'in- chi- - na.
-cer〉 ce- de e s'in- chi- na, ce- de e s'in- chi- - na.
-cer〉 ce- de e s'in- chi- na, ce- de e s'in- chi- - na.
6 5 9 8 4 3 6 5 4 3
81
Terza parte
El- la si re- ca a sde- gno Di sa- lu- tar l'au- ro- ra E l'au- ra,
El- la si re- ca a sde- gno Di sa- lu- tar l'au- ro-
Di sa- lu- tar l'au-
86
Di sa- lu- tar l'au- ro- ra E l'au- ra, si re- ca a sde-
-ra, 〈Di sa- lu- tar l'au- ro- ra〉 E l'au- ra, Di sa- lu- tar l'au- ro- ra, si
-ro- ra, 〈Di sa- lu- tar l'au- ro- ra〉 E l'au- ra,
Di sa- lu- tar l'au- ro- ra E l'au- ra, El- la,
5 6 5 6 5 6

90
-gno Di sa- lu- tar l'au- ro- ra E l'au- ra, Di sa- lu- tar l'au- ro- ra, ⟨Di
re- ca a sde- gno Di sa- lu- tar l'au- ro- ra E l'au- ra, Di sa- lu- tar l'au-
Di sa- lu- tar l'au- ro- ra E l'au- ra, Di sa- lu- tar l'au- ro-
el- la si re- ca a sde- gno
94
sa- lu- tar l'au- ro- ra⟩ E l'au- ra, che col gior- no Dal mar e-
-ro- ra E l'au- ra, che col gior- no Dal mar e- sco- no
- ra E l'au- ra, che col gior- no Dal mar e- sco- no
Di sa- lu- tar l'au- ro- ra E l'au- ra, che col gior- no Dal mar e- sco- no
99
- sco- no fuo- ra; So- lo sa- lu- ta il sol,
fuo- ra; sa- lu- ta il sol, ⟨sa- lu- ta il
fuo- ra; sa- lu- ta il sol, sa- lu- ta il sol,
fuo- ra; So- lo,
4 3

105
sa- lu- ta il sol, sa- lu- ta il sol, ⟨sa- lu- ta il
sol,⟩ sa- lu- ta il sol, sa- lu- ta il sol
⟨sa- lu- ta il sol, sa- lu- ta il sol⟩
so- lo sa- lu- ta il sol, sa- - lu- ta il
110
sol⟩ e vol ch'i ven- - ti Tac- - cia- no al suon de'
e vol ch'i ven- - ti Tac- - cia- no al suon de'
e vol ch'i ven- - ti Tac- - cia- no al suon de'
sol e vol ch'i ven- - ti Tac- - cia- no al suon
116
suoi so- a- vi ac- cen- - ti, e vol ch'i ven-
suoi so- a- vi ac- cen- - ti, e vol ch'i ven-
suoi so- a- vi ac- cen- - ti, e vol ch'i ven-
e vol ch'i ven-

122
- ti Tac- - cia- no al suon
- ti Tac- - cia- no al suon de' suoi so-
- ti Tac- - cia- no al suon de' suoi so-
- ti Tac- - cia- no al suon de' suoi so-
128
de' suoi so- a-
-a- vi ac- cen- - ti,
-a- vi ac- cen- - ti, de' suoi so-
-a- vi ac- cen- - ti, de' suoi so-
133
- vi ac- cen- ti, so- a vi ac- cen- ti.
de' suoi so- a- vi ac- cen- - ti.
-a- vi ac- cen- - - - ti.
-a- vi ac- cen- - - - ti.

Quarta parte

139

El- la gli a- gri- col- to- ri   Chia- ma con cer- ta
Chia- ma con cer- ta spe- ne, El- la gli a- gri- col- to- ri,
El- la gli a- gri- col- to- ri Chia- ma con cer- ta spe- ne, con cer- ta
Chia- ma con cer- ta spe- ne, El- la gli a- gri- col-

144

spe- ne, Chia- ma con cer- ta spe- ne,
El- la gli a- gri- col- to- ri Chia- ma con cer- ta spe-
spe- ne, Chia- ma con cer- ta spe- ne, con cer- ta spe- ne, El- la gli a-
-to- ri, El- la gli a- gri- col- to- ri Chia- ma con

149

⟨Chia- ma con cer- ta spe- ne⟩ E ne gli e- sti-
-ne, con cer- ta spe- ne E ne gli e- sti-
-gri- col- to- ri Chia- ma con cer- ta spe- ne E ne gli e- sti-
cer- ta spe- ne E ne gli e- sti-

154
- vi ar- do- ri Col can- - to gl'in- trat- tie-
- vi ar- do- ri Col can- to, col can- - to gl'in- trat- tie-
- vi ar- do- ri Col can- - - to gl'in- trat- tie-
- vi ar- do- ri
6
[♯]
159
-ne, E ne gli e- sti- - vi ar- do- ri
-ne, E ne gli e- sti- - vi ar- do- ri Col can- -
-ne, E ne gli e- sti- - vi ar- do- ri Col can- to, col can-
E ne gli e- sti- - vi ar- do- ri Col can- -
6
[♮]
164
Pro- met- ten- do ad o- gnor di
-to gl'in- trat- tie- ne, Pro- met- ten- do ad o- gnor di
- to gl'in- trat- tie- ne, Pro- met- ten- do ad o- gnor di
- to gl'in- trat- tie- ne, Pro- met- ten- do ad o- gnor di
[♯]
[♯]
[♮]

169
ren- der lo- - ro Nel- le do- ra- te spi- - ghe il se- col
ren- der lo- ro Nel- le do- ra- te spi- ghe, nel- le do-
ren- der lo- ro Nel- le do- ra- te spi- ghe il se- col d'o- ro, Nel- le do-
ren- der lo- ro Nel- le do- ra- te spi- ghe il
[♮]6 6 6 5 6
174
d'o- ro, il se- col d'o- ro, Pro- met- ten- do ad o-
-ra- te spi- ghe il se- col d'o- ro, Pro- met- ten- do ad o-
-ra- te spi- ghe il se- col d'o- - ro, Pro- met- ten- do ad o-
se- col d'o- ro, il se- col d'o- ro, Pro- met- ten- do ad o-
5 6 ♭ 4 3 6
179
-gnor, ⟨pro- met- ten- do ad o- gnor,⟩ di ren- der lo- ro
-gnor, ⟨pro- met- ten- do ad o- gnor,⟩ di ren- der lo- - ro
-gnor, ⟨pro- met- ten- do ad o- gnor,⟩ di ren- der lo- ro
-gnor, ⟨pro- met- ten- do ad o- gnor,⟩ di ren- der lo- ro Nel- le do-
6 7 6

Nelle dorate spighe, nelle dorate spighe, (nelle dorate spighe,) il secol d'oro.

Quinta parte

Ma non ha san-
È ver ch'in terra nasce,

198
- - gue, non ha san- gue e
- gue, ⟨ma non ha san- gue,⟩ non ha san- gue
Ma non ha san- - - gue
Ma non ha san- gue
203
so- lo Di ru- gia- da si pa- sce, ⟨Di ru- gia- da si pa-
e so- lo Di ru- gia- da si pa- sce, Di ru- gia- da si pa- sce,
e so- lo Di ru- gia- da si pa-
e so- lo
208
-sce,⟩ Di ru- gia- da si pa- sce, ⟨Di ru- gia- da si pa- sce,⟩
e so- lo Di ru- gia- da si pa- sce, Di ru-
-sce, e so- lo Di ru- gia- da
Di ru- gia- da si pa- sce, ⟨Di ru- gia- da si

212

e so- lo Di ru- gia- da si pa- - sce; Da lei fug- ge o-gni

-gia- da si pa- - sce, ⟨Di ru- gia- da si pa- - sce;⟩ Da lei fug- ge o-gni

— si pa- - sce, ⟨Di ru- gia- da si pa- - sce;⟩ Da lei fug- ge o-gni

pa- - sce,⟩ Di ru- gia- da si pa- sce; Da lei fug- ge o-gni

6 5 7 6

217

do- - lo: Vi- ve sen- za ti- mor, ⟨vi-

do- - lo: Vi- ve sen- za ti- mor, ⟨vi-

do- - lo: Vi- ve sen- za ti- mor, ⟨vi-

do- - lo: Vi- ve sen- za ti- mor, ⟨vi-

7 6 4 3 ♭

222

-ve sen- za ti- mor,⟩ so- lo ha di ma- le, di ma-

-ve sen- za ti- mor,⟩ so- lo ha di ma-

-ve sen- za ti- mor,⟩ so- lo ha di ma- -

-ve sen- za ti- mor,⟩

4 3 7 [♮]6

227
-le, so- lo ha di ma- le
-le, so- lo ha di ma- - le Che mo- stra
-le, so- lo ha di ma- - le Che mo- - stra col
so- lo ha di ma- le Che mo- stra col
7 [♮]6 4 3 5 5 2
233
Che mo- stra
col mo- rir, che mo- - stra col
mo- rir, ⟨che mo- stra col mo-
mo- rir d'es-
6 ♯ 6 5 9
239
col mo- rir d'es- - ser mor- ta- -
mo- rir, col mo- rir d'es- - ser mor-
-rir⟩ d'es- - ser mor- ta- le, d'es- - ser
- ser mor- ta- - le,
3 4 3 9 8 4 3

245
- - le, d'es- ser mor-
-ta- le, d'es- - ser mor- - ta-
mor- - ta- - le, ⟨d'es- ser mor-
d'es- - ser mor- ta-
4 3 6
251
Sesta ed ultima parte
-ta- le. Il mon- do, dun- que‿a- vam-
- le. Il mon- do, dun- que‿a- vam- pi, Il
-ta- le.⟩ Il mon- do, dun- que‿a- vam- pi,
- le. Il
5 6
256
- pi, a- - vam- pi, Pur- - ché tu can- -
mon- do, dun- que‿a-vam- pi, Pur- - ché tu can- - ti, tu
⟨Il mon- do, dun- que‿a-vam- pi,⟩ Pur- - ché tu can- - ti, tu
mon- do, dun- que‿a- vam- pi, Pur- - ché tu can- -
5 6

261
- ti sem- pre, Si- re- net- ta de' cam- pi, Si- re-
can- ti sem- pre, Si- re- net- ta de' cam- pi, Si- re-
can- ti sem- pre, Si- re- net- ta de' cam-
- ti sem- pre, Si- re- net- ta de' cam-
265
-net- ta de' cam- - - pi, ⟨Si- re- net- ta de' cam-
-net- ta de' cam- pi, Si- re- net- ta de' cam- pi, ⟨Si- re-
-pi, Si- re- net- ta de' cam- pi, ⟨Si- re- net- ta de' cam-
-pi, Si- re- net- ta de' cam- pi, Si- re-
6
269
-pi,⟩ de' cam- pi; Par- mi d'u- dir tem- prar al dio di
-net- ta de' cam- pi;⟩ Ch'u- den- do le tue tem- pre Par- mi d'u-
- pi;⟩ Ch'u- den- do le tue tem- pre
-net- ta de' cam- pi; Ch'u- den- do le tue tem- pre,
6 4 3 5 6 6 6 6

274
De- lo, Ch'u- den- do le tue tem- - pre
-dir tem- prar al dio di De- - lo, di De- lo, Ch'u- den- do le tue
Par- mi d'u-dir tem- prar al dio di De- lo, Par- - mi d'u- dir tem- prar al dio di
Ch'u- den- do le tue tem- pre Par- mi d'u-dir tem- prar al dio di
6 7 [♮]6 6
279
Par- mi d'u- dir tem- prar al dio di De- lo,
tem- pre Par- - mi d'u- dir tem- - prar, par- mi d'u-
De- lo, Ch'u- den- do le tue tem- pre, le tue tem-
De- lo, Par- mi d'u- dir tem- prar al
7 6 6 ♮
283
Par- mi d'u- dir tem- prar al dio di De- -
-dir tem- prar al dio di De- lo, al dio di De-
- pre Par- mi d'u- dir tem- prar al dio di De-
dio di De- lo
6 6 7 [♯]6 4 3

287
-lo con l'ar- mo- nia del cie-
-lo Il can- - to suo con l'ar- mo- nia del cie-
-lo Il can- - to suo con l'ar- mo- nia del cie-
Il can- - to suo, il
291
-lo, Il can- - to suo con l'ar- mo- nia del cie- lo, con
-lo, Il can- - to suo con l'ar- mo- nia del cie-
-lo, Il can- - to suo con l'ar- mo- nia del cie-
can- - to suo con l'ar- mo- nia del cie-
295
l'ar- - mo- nia del cie- - lo.
-lo, con l'ar- - mo- nia del cie- lo.
-lo, con l'ar- - mo- nia, con l'ar- mo- nia del cie- lo.
-lo, con l'ar- - mo- nia del cie- lo.

27. Litaniae Beatae Mariae Virginis

17
-ri- e e- le- i- son.
-le- - - - - i- son.
-le- i- son.
7 6 4 3
23
Pa- ter de cae- lis De- us, mi-
Pa- ter de cae- lis De- - us, mi-
Pa- ter de cae- lis De- - us, mi-
6 4 3
28
-se- re- re no- -
- - se- re- re no- -
- se- re- - re no- -
5 6 7 6 4 3

Sheet music, lyrics:

-bis. Fi-li Re-demptor mun-di Deus, mi-se-re-re no-bis. Spi-ri-tus sancte De-

49
-us, mi- - se- re- re no-
-us, mi- se- re- - - re no-
-us, mi- - se- re- - re no-
5 6 6 4 3
54
-bis. San- - cta Tri- ni- tas u- - nus
-bis. San- cta Tri- ni- tas
-bis. San- cta Tri- ni- tas u-
6 5 ♯
60
De- us, u- - nus De- us, mi- se- re-
u- nus De- - - us, mi- se- re-
-nus De- - - us, mi- se- re-
6 5 5 6 4 3 6

66
- re no- bis. San- cta Ma-
- re no- bis. San- - cta Ma- - ri-
- re no- bis. San- cta Ma-
72
-ri- - a, o-
- - a, o- ra
-ri- - a, o- ra pro
77
-ra pro no- -
pro no- bis, pro no- -
no- bis, o- ra pro no-

82
-bis. San- - cta De- i Ge- ni- trix, o- - ra pro
-bis. San- - cta De- i Ge- ni- trix, o- ra pro no-
-bis. San- - cta De- i Ge- ni- trix, o- ra pro
88
no- bis. San- cta Vir- go Vir- gi- num, o-
- - bis. San- cta Vir- go Vir- gi- num, o-
no- bis. San- cta Vir- go Vir- gi- num, o-
93
-ra pro no- bis. Ma- -
- ra pro no- - bis. Ma- -
-ra pro no- - bis. Ma-

98
- ter Chri- - sti, o- ra
- ter Chri- - sti, o-
- - ter Chri- sti, o- ra
103
pro no- - bis.
-ra [pro no- bis. Ma- ter di- vi-]
pro no- bis. Ma- ter di-
109
Ma- ter di- vi- nae gra- ti- ae, o-
- nae gra- ti- ae, o- ra pro no- bis, pro
-vi- nae gra- ti- ae, o- ra pro no-

141

132
-ma, o- ra pro no- bis. Ma- ter in- vi- o-
pro no- - bis. Ma-
no- - - bis. Ma- ter in-
4 3 5 6 4 3
138
-la- ta, o- ra pro no-
-ter in- vi- o- la- ta, o- ra pro
-vi- o- la- ta, o- ra pro
5 [♮]6
143
- - bis. Ma- ter in- te- me- ra-
no- - bis. Ma- ter in- te- me- ra-
no- - bis. Ma- ter in- te- me- ra-
4 [♭]3 4 3 6 [♭]

149
-ta, o- ra pro no-
-ta, o- ra pro no-
-ta, o- ra pro no- -
154
- bis. o-
- bis. Ma- ter ad- - mi- ra- - bi- lis, o-
- bis. Ma- ter ad- - mi- ra- bi- lis, o-
160
-ra pro no- bis. Vir- go ve- ne- ran- da et prae- di-
-ra pro no- bis. Vir- go ve- ne- ran- da et prae- di-
-ra pro no- bis. Vir- go ve- ne- ran- da et prae- di-

166
-can- da, o- ra pro no- bis. Vir- go- pru-
-can- da, o- ra pro no- bis.
-can- da, o- ra pro no- bis. Vir-
172
- - den- tis- - - si- ma, o-
o- ra pro
-go pru- - - den- tis- si- ma,
178
-ra pro no- - - bis. Se-
no- - - - bis. Se-
Se-

-des sa- pi- en- ti- ae, o- ra pro no- bis.

Cau- sa no- strae lae- ti- ti- ae, o- ra pro no-

-bis. Do- mus au- - re-

198
o- ra pro no- bis. Stel- la ma- tu- ti-
-a, o- ra pro no- bis. Stel- la ma- tu- ti-
-a, o- ra pro no- bis. Stel- la ma- tu- ti-
204
-na, o- ra pro no- bis. Sa- lus in-
-na, o- ra pro no- bis. Sa- - lus in- -
-na, o- ra pro no- bis. Sa- lus in-
210
- fir- mo- rum, Re- fu- gi- um pec-
- fir- mo- rum, o- ra pro no- bis. Re- fu- gi- um pec-
- fir- mo- rum, o- ra pro no- bis. Re- fu- gi- um pec-

216
- ca- to- rum, o- ra pro no- bis, o- ra pro no-
- ca- to- rum, o- ra pro no- bis.
- ca- to- rum, o- ra pro no- bis, o- ra pro no-
221
-bis. Con- - so- - la- - trix af-
Con- - so- la- trix af-
-bis. Con- - so- la- trix af-
6
226
- fli- cto- - rum, o- ra pro no-
-fli- cto- - rum, o- ra pro no-
- fli- cto- - rum, o- ra pro no-
6 7 6 4 3

231
-bis. Au- xi- li- um Chri- sti- a- no- - rum, o-
-bis. Au- xi- li- um Chri- sti- a- no- rum, o-
-bis. Au- xi- li- um Chri- sti- a- no- rum,
235
-ra pro no- - - bis.
-ra pro no- - - bis.
o- ra pro no- bis.
239
O3
Re- gi- na An- ge- lo- rum, o- ra pro no-
Re- gi- na An- ge- lo- rum, o- ra pro no-
o- ra pro no-

244
-bis. Re- gi- na Pa- tri- ar- cha- rum et Pro- phe-
-bis. Re- gi- na Pa- tri- ar- cha- rum et Pro- phe-
-bis. Re- gi- na Pa- tri- ar- cha- rum et Pro- phe-
249
-ta- rum, o- ra pro no- bis. Re-
-ta- rum, o- ra pro no- bis. Re-
-ta- rum, o- ra pro no- - bis. Re-
254
-gi- na A- po- sto- lo- rum, o- ra pro no-
-gi- na A- po- sto- - lo- rum, o- ra pro no-
-gi- na A- po- sto- lo- rum, o- ra pro no-

259
-bis. Re- gi- na Mar- ty- rum et Con- fes- so- rum,
-bis. Re- gi- na Mar- ty- rum et Con- fes- so- rum,
-bis. Re- gi- na Mar- ty- rum et Con- fes- so- rum,
264
o- ra pro no- bis. Re- gi- na Vir- gi- num, o- ra pro
o- ra pro no- bis. Re- gi- na Vir- gi- num, o- ra pro
o- ra pro no- bis. Re- gi- na Vir- gi- num, o- ra pro
269
C
no- bis. Re- gi- na San- cto- rum om- ni-
no- bis. Re- gi- na San- cto- rum om- ni-
no- bis. Re- gi- - na San- cto- rum om- ni-

274
-um, o- ra pro no- - bis.
-um, o- ra pro no- bis.
-um, o- ra pro no- - bis.
279
A- - gnus De- - - i, qui tol- lis pec-
A- - gnus De- i, qui tol- lis pec-
A- - gnus De- i, qui tol- lis pec-
285
-ca- ta mun- di, par- - ce, par- -
-ca- ta mun- di, par- - - ce
-ca- ta mun- di, par- - - -

-ce no- bis Do- mi- ne. A- gnus
no- bis Do- mi- ne. A- gnus
-ce no- bis Do- mi- ne. A- gnus

De- i, qui tol- lis pec- ca- ta mun- di, ex-
De- i, qui tol- lis pec- ca- ta mun- di,
De- i, qui tol- lis pec- ca- ta mun- di, ex-

- au- di nos
ex- au- di nos
au- di nos Do-

307
Do- - mi- ne. A- - gnus De-
Do- - mi- ne. A- - gnus De-
- - mi- ne. A- - gnus De-
4 [♮]3 ♮ ♯
313
-i, qui tol- lis pec- ca- ta mun- di, mi- - se-
-i, qui tol- lis pec- ca- ta mun- di,
-i, qui tol- lis pec- ca- ta mun- di, mi-
[♯] ♯ ♯
319
- re- - - re no- - bis.
mi- se- re- re no- - bis.
-se- re- - re no- - bis.
6 4 3

Critical Report

Sources

The title page of the *Selva armonica* (RISM A 1122; *NV* 75), framed by a decoration bearing the partbook specification, reads as follows (see pl. 1):

> SELVA ARMONICA. | DOVE | SI CONTENGONO | Motetti, Madrigali, Canzonette, | Dialogi, Arie, à una, doi, | tre, & quattro voci. | DI GIO. FRANCESCO ANERIO ROMANO, | Maestro di Cappella della Madonna Santissima | delli Monti di Roma. | [Avila family coat of arms] | IN ROMA, Appresso Gio:Battista Robletti. 1617. | [rule] | CON LICENZA DE' SUPERIORI.

The print consists of three partbooks (162 x 212 mm): Canto, Basso et Tenore, and Basso dell'organo (a number of pieces call for additional parts, including canto secondo, alto, and baritono; these parts and sometimes the tenore are printed in the Canto partbook). Each partbook bears the dedication to Isabella Avila on page 2 (see pl. 2). The print is generally reliable and corruptions are rare, although inaccuracies in the typesetting are not completely absent. Moreover, the modern editor has to face the usual negligence in the graphic presentation of the literary text. The present edition is based on the complete partbook set in the Biblioteca del Conservatorio di Santa Cecilia (pressmark G.Cs.1.A.20$^{4-7}$; previously belonging to the Biblioteca Angelica).[1] A second complete copy, held in the Biblioteca Vallicelliana in Rome (pressmark VI.15.B.39), has been systematically examined as well. An incomplete copy is preserved in the library of the Accademia Chigiana in Siena.

Editorial Methods

Part names are given in Italian or Latin according to the original print. The works appear in their original order but are numbered editorially. Most titles are based on the first phrase, line, or sometimes the first two lines of the texts. The only exception is "Litaniae Beatae Mariae Virginis" (no. 27), which is titled in the print according to the genre of the prayer it sets; the most complete form of its title appears in the canto primo, canto secondo, and basso parts, and this form has been used as the title in the edition. Musical genre labels, when present in the partbooks, are shown as subtitles in the edition. The original clef, key signature, mensuration sign, first notated pitch, and any preceding rests in each voice part is shown in an incipit at the beginning of each work. The range of each voice is shown after the modern clef, key signature, and meter signature, indicating the range of pitches as they appear in the modern clef. In the case of the *coro* in "O tu, che vai per via" (no. 23), which enters near the end of the piece, the original clefs and voice ranges are given in the critical notes.

Performance indications that strictly pertain to the partbook format, such as "A due," "Tacet," and the like, are tacitly omitted. Most pieces include rubrics that describe the voicing of the setting. In the thirteen solos, rubrics range from the indication "solo" in the Canto partbook to the more complete "canto solo ovvero tenore solo," which usually appears in the Basso dell'organo partbook. Because these rubrics apply to all solos (see "Notes on Performance" in the introduction), they have been omitted in the edition and the options for the soloist's voice type (i.e., canto or tenore) discussed under "Notes on Performance" in the introduction. In other pieces, the written indications sometimes provide performance guidelines that pertain only to one particular piece, and in these cases the rubrics are recorded in the critical notes in their most complete form. Footnotes in the edition direct performers to the critical notes when the rubrics give significant performance options.

Beaming and stem direction have been tacitly modernized. Barlines are inserted after each basic unit, and notes that continue past a barline in the transcription are divided into appropriate values and connected with a tie. The measures are numbered continuously through all parts of the compositions in more than one part, with double barlines distinguishing each part. The last note of each section is provided with a fermata. Ligatures and coloration are shown by full and open horizontal brackets, respectively. Apart from "Torna la sera bruna" (no. 21), notated entirely in coloration (see below), coloration is usually introduced to represent a succession of imperfect values in a ternary context. "Ecco che i monti indora" (no. 16, mm. 111 and 123) includes the only instance of coloration used to indicate a triplet.

Repeats indicate an AABB form in a number of the compositions or their internal parts. They are originally indicated by the sign ·ǁ· for the first half (A) and by the insertion of the first words to be repeated for the second (B). The first part of "O dolce amor, Gesù" (no. 4) is the only case where repetitions create the form AABCC (here the textual recall refers to a point several measures beyond the ‖·). Repeats are rendered in accordance with modern usage. In "La matutina aurora" (no. 7, *Terza parte*) and "Ecco riede, ecco soggiorna" (no. 8), the repetition occurring within a measure has required the insertion of first and second endings in accordance with modern usage.

The edition retains the original note values in duple meter passages, and the original meter C has been consistently transcribed as $\frac{2}{2}$. In triple meter passages, the original signatures O3, C3, and 3 are all represented by $\frac{3}{4}$, and note values have been reduced by a half or a quarter, depending on context; quadripartition of the values is applied when the ternary perfection is originally on the breve level (as is usually the case), bipartition when the perfection is on the semibreve level (in "Dal tuo volto beato" [no. 2] only). "Torna la sera bruna" (no. 21) is the only piece notated entirely in triple time; the meter is achieved through a comprehensive coloration (clearly an instance of *Augenmusik*) and the use of the dotted colored semibreve as a perfect value. Here too bipartition is applied in the edition.

Reducing the note values in triple meter passages renders an orientation from which performers can develop appropriate mensural relationships as they shift between duple and triple meters; for example, triple meter sections are sometimes characterized by virtuosic figuration, a feature that the original long note values can visually obscure (see "La matutina aurora" [no. 7], mm. 53ff.).[2] The problem of horizontal tempo relationships among various meters in the performance of late sixteenth- and early seventeenth-century music has been widely discussed in the last decades. Some scholars believe that the shift from duple to triple meter must rigidly follow the proportional ratio indicated by the sign. Roger Bowers, for instance, proposes to maintain for the tripla a ratio of 3:1 on the semibreve level (e.g., C ◊ = C3◊ ◊ ◊), accepting the authority of Adriano Banchieri—who quotes an example by Giovanni Francesco Anerio on this very subject.[3] According to this hypothesis, the modern whole note of $\frac{2}{2}$ in our edition would be equivalent to the dotted half of the following $\frac{3}{4}$; thus the quarter note would become one third longer ($\frac{2}{2}$ o = $\frac{3}{4}$ ♩.; $\frac{2}{2}$ ♩♩♩♩ = $\frac{3}{4}$ ♩♩♩).

A less rigid opinion, supported, e.g., by Uwe Wolf,[4] has won wider acceptance. This line of thought dismisses the necessity of strict proportionalism, allowing triple time sections to be faster than under strict proportionalism and to maintain a steady basic beat between duple and triple time sections, features that seem appropriate to the overall rhythmic structure of Anerio's writing. In this perspective, the duration of all note values remains constant in the modern transcription (not $\frac{2}{2}$ o = $\frac{3}{4}$ ♩. but, going directly to the quarter note, $\frac{2}{2}$ ♩ = $\frac{3}{4}$ ♩). Because the relationship between duple and triple sections is, to a certain extent, a matter of interpretation, however, performers are encouraged to make their choice within the range defined by these two approaches. When the signature changes within a piece, the edition shows the original signature above the top staff (with any discrepancy among the parts recorded in the critical notes), but no equivalences have been suggested.

All accidentals from the source are retained in the edition, including those that are cautionary or redundant by modern practice. Editorial accidentals are placed on the staff in brackets, and have been added (1) to cancel a source accidental that is no longer valid when a previously inflected note recurs later in the same measure; (2) to clarify that a source accidental applies across a barline; and (3) to match an inflection that is present or required by the continuo figures. Figures appear as they do in the source, except that they are consistently placed above the staff and their positions slightly adjusted to occur on metrically strong beats. Figures are spaced evenly over sustained bass notes unless they are clearly analogues to melodic motion in the voice, in which case they align with the voice (performers may alter the placement of certain figures in their realizations, especially for "4–3" cadence ornamentations, the actual timing of which depends on agreement among performers—see note 63 in the introduction). The figures "4–3" imply a major chord unless an editorial sign warns that the third is minor. Editorial additions are supplied in square brackets only when they help to clarify an otherwise ambiguous harmony, match a parallel passage, or correspond to an inflection in the voices. Sharps (in the two forms ♯ and 𝄪) and flats are transcribed as naturals when appropriate in accordance with modern usage in both the accidentals and continuo figures.

"Dio ti salvi, Maria, Madre divina" (no. 22) is the only composition originally written in the so-called *chiavette* (with the canto part in G2 clef). The corresponding continuo part (in C3 clef) bears the indication "alla quarta," calling for a transposition down a fourth. By comparison, the three pieces where the continuo is in C4 clef ("Ecco vien fuor la notte," [no. 18], "Occhi del cielo ardenti," [no. 19], and "Litaniae Beatae Mariae Virginis" [no. 27]) bear the indication "sonate come sta" (play as it stands, i.e., at the original pitch level). Because the source clearly requires transposition to achieve the proper pitch level, "Dio ti salvi, Maria, Madre divina" (no. 22) has been transposed down a fourth in the edition and the key signature added to preserve the original intervals.

Editorial policies regarding the texts are discussed in the "Texts and Translations" section. The fairly accurate text underlay of the print has seldom required rearrangements, but significant adjustments are indicated in the critical notes. Words are divided according to modern rules of Italian and Latin syllabification. Repetitions of text shown in the original by an idem sign are enclosed in angle brackets in the edition. Missing text has been added editorially in square brackets. The capital at the beginning of a poetic line is retained whenever a full poetic line is repeated.

Critical Notes

The critical notes record discrepancies between the source and the edition. Notes are located by measure number, part name, and the note within the measure on which they occur, counting tied noteheads separately. Notes reporting emendations to spelling may identify the original reading by beat within the measure. The following abbreviations are employed in the critical notes: C = canto, C1 = canto primo/cantus primus, C2 = canto secondo/cantus secundus, A = alto, T = tenore, Bar = baritono, B = basso/bassus, B. org. = basso dell'organo, sbr = semibreve, min = minim, smin = semiminim, sfusa = semifusa. Pitches are given according to the system in which middle C = c'.

1. *Sommo Re delle stelle*

Mm. 52–53, C, the originally ambiguous underlay of the syllables "E a la sua de-" has been rearranged. M. 60, C, note 5 (tied to note 1 in m. 61) is smin.

3. *Il tempo passa e mai più si ritrova*

M. 36, B. org., note 1, figure added based on the parallel passage. M. 57, B. org., note 2, figure added based on the parallel passage.

4. *O dolce amor, Gesù*

Mm. 5 and 8, B. org., figures are on the staff (before the notes) rather than above it. M. 13, C, note 1 is smin. M. 37, B. org., note 3, figures are inverted (5–6). M. 97, B. org., figures are inverted (5–6).

5. *Acerbe doglie e voi, piaghe amorose*

M. 26, C, note 4 is sfusa. Mm. 65, note 2 to m. 71, C, text is "aspro e penoso."

6. *Donna celeste, che di Dio sei Madre*

The initial meter signs are conflicting, as shown in the incipit.

7. *La matutina aurora*

M. 30, C, syllables "-da l'o-" are set to notes 1 and 2; altered based on the parallel passage in m. 36. M. 41, B. org., note 2 is smin. M. 91, B. org., note 1 is min.

8. *Ecco riede, ecco soggiorna*

The instrumental ritornello is printed on a slip of paper pasted on the page of the B. org. partbook. M. 11, C, note 4 is min.

9. *Pulchra es*

M. 38, B. org., note 1, figure 5 is over note 2. M. 104, B. org., meter is O3. M. 121, B. org., note is min.

11. *Regina caeli*

M. 38, B. org., measure is missing; added conjecturing a haplographic error.

12. *Ego flos campi*

Mm. 37–39, C, text is "filias."

13. *Salve, Regina*

Titled "Salve, Latina" in the *Tavola* and B. org. partbook, indicating that the text is in Latin, to distinguish the piece from the one following.

14. *Salve Regina, Madre divina*

Titled "Salve Regina volgare" in the *Tavola* and C partbook, indicating that the text is an Italian version of the Latin antiphon. The rubric in the partbooks explains that the piece may be sung by canto *solo* or by canto and basso together. The most complete version is in the B. org. partbook, reading: "Canto solo, et a 2 si placet, cioè Canto e Basso." M. 56, C, text underlay has been conformed to that of the B, contracting "-gi a" to a single syllable (synalepha) and placing it on note 5. M. 76, B. org., note 2 has figure ♯. M. 78, B, notes 2–3 are sfusas.

15. *Gesù, nel tuo partire*

The rubric in the partbooks explains that the piece may be sung by two cantos or by canto and tenore, the tenore reading the C2 part an octave lower. The most complete version is in the B. org. partbook, reading: "A due Canti, ovvero Canto e Tenore, cantando però un Soprano all'ottava bassa." M. 20, B. org., note 3, the figure 6 is on note 1 of m. 21.

16. *Ecco che i monti indora*

M. 30, B. org., note 2 has figure ♯. M. 94, C2, meter is 3.

17. *Alta cosa è il mio Dio*

Mm. 1 and 6, T, text is "Altra" (the correct text appears on a slip of paper pasted into the Biblioteca Vallicelliana exemplar). M. 16, B. org., note 3 is f. Mm. 28–29, T, text is "core." M. 30, B. org., meter is O3. M. 74, C, note 1, text is "il." M. 107, T, notes 2–3, text is "ess'io."

18. *Ecco vien fuor la notte*

The rubric in the B. org. partbook reads, "Sonate come sta," indicating that the pitches should sound as written. M. 2, B. org., note 2 has figure ♯. M. 5, C2, note 2, text is "dal." M. 11, C2, note 3, text is "che in." M. 12, C2, notes 2–3, text is "-zo a l'ombre." M. 41, T, note 3 is min. M. 57, C2, underlay of the word "onore" (with the syllable "-no" originally related to note 4) has been conformed to the parallel passage at m. 47.

19. *Occhi del cielo ardenti*

The rubric in the B. org. partbook reads, "Sonate come sta," indicating that the pitches should sound as written. M. 4, C1, note 3 is smin. M. 34, C1 and C2, text is "Scoperto i." M. 37, C2, note 2 to m. 38, note 1, text is "ch'all'un." Mm. 48–52, among various possible text underlay solutions, it seems preferable to put a *dialepha* between "fa" and "i" and to read "suoi" as a monosyllable. M. 65–68, C1, text is "Nel ciel lucente." M. 75, C1, note 3 to m. 76, notes 1–2, text is "Acciochè" (one word). Mm. 94 and 96, C1, notes 2–3, text is "viver."

20. *Alzate al sommo ciel memoria e mente*

M. 1, C1, note 5 is smin. M. 21, C1, note 1 to m. 23, note 1, text is "benedite." Mm. 47–50, B. org. reads as in example 1; emendation based on the B line. M. 48, B, note 2, syllable is "-ste." M. 50, B, note 2, text is "Sii il."

M. 121, C1 and B, notes 4–5, syllables are "-gon i." M. 127, B. org., meter is O3. M. 131, B, note 2 to m. 132, note 2, text is "laud'io." M. 164, C2, notes 1–2, text is "noti e." M. 164, C2, note 3 to m. 165, note 2, text is "consonante" (one word). M. 171, C1, note 4, text is "de."

Example 1.

B. org. [musical notation]

21. *Torna la sera bruna*

A comprehensive coloration is adopted, without any mensuration sign (only C1, *Quinta parte*, bears the usual c). Only the notes in the second endings are uncolored (mm. 23, 46, 69, 92, and 117). An alternative baritono part appears in a separate section of the Canto partbook. Editorial figures in the B. org. have been added based on parallel passages in other *partes*. M. 11, Bar and B, note 1, text is "Ch'il." M. 24, Bar, text is "salvami." M. 83, B, note 2 to m. 86, note 2, a slip of paper is pasted on page 29 of the Basso et tenore partbook to emend the text underlay.

22. *Dio ti salvi, Maria, Madre divina*

The rubric "Alla quarta" indicates that this piece, written in *chiavette*, must be transposed down a fourth in performance; the transposition has been undertaken in the edition. M. 32, B. org., no meter change is indicated. M. 38, C2, note 1 is sbr. M. 56, C2, note 2 is e". M. 58, C1 and Bar, beat 4, text is "de." M. 72, C2 and A, note 3 to m. 73, text is "mia." (a handwritten emendation in the copy held at the Biblioteca Vallicelliana corrects the text). M. 74, C1, meter is 3.

23. *O tu, che vai per via*

For parts that rest before entering, incipits show only the rest immediately before the first sounding pitch. M. 40, C, because of a typographical error, the min rest (anomalously printed on the first line of the staff) is misplaced *within* the melodic phrase, instead of preceding it. M. 105, *coro* section, the original clef and modern ranges are as follows: C = C1 clef, range d'–d"; A = C3 clef, range g–a'; T = C4 clef, range g–f'; B = F4 clef, range G–c'.

24. *O del gran Redentor Madre alma e bella*

The B. org. partbook bears the indication, "A 4. Voci ordinarie" (probably because of the particular structure of the previous dialogo). M. 27, C, note 1 is e", note 2 is a'. M. 109, B. org., note 2, a figure 7 precedes the 6.

26. *Io non saprei dir quanto*

M. 98, A, note 3 is c'. M. 113, C, to m. 114, note 3, text is "Taccian al." M. 125, B, text is "son." M. 150, B. org. has figures 4–3; moved to m. 151 in the edition. M. 186, B. org., figures are misplaced (note 1 has 6–5, note 3 only 6). M. 212, B. org., note 1, figures are 7–6. M. 250, A, text underlay has been rearranged (syllable "-ta-" is under note 4 in m. 249). M. 264, C, note 3 is smin. M. 287, T, note 5 is b♭. M. 291, T, note 4 is c, note 5 is B♭. M. 292, A, note 4 is e'.

27. *Litaniae Beatae Mariae Virginis*

The rubric in the B. org. partbook reads, "Sonate come sta," indicating that the pitches should sound as written. The B. org. part bears the indication "2 canti e baritono," but the vocal part is named "bassus." In the title, which appears in various versions in all the partbooks, "Beatae" is abbreviated as "B." The final "Agnus" is distinguished from the previous section by the insertion of an initial capital (except in the B. org., which uses a double barline). The text underlay in the Kyrie has been substantially rearranged because of the lack of syllabication. Some slips of paper bearing printed original corrections are pasted on pages 57–59 of the B part; a similar though smaller intervention is made in C1, m. 175, where note 2 is printed on another slip of paper.

M. 114, C1, note is g'. M. 166, C2, the syllable "-can" is under note 3. M. 179, B. org. has figures 4–3; moved to m. 181 in the edition. M. 188, C2 and B, meter is 3. M. 191, B. org., note 1 has the figure ✕ instead of 5. M. 193, B. org., note (tied to note in m. 194) is sbr. M. 291, C1, note 2 is f'. M. 308, B, note 1, the ♯ appears before note 2 of m. 307.

Notes

1. Signatures in the partbooks appear in the following order: Canto—A2, B, B2, C, C2, D, D2, E, E2, F, F2, G, G2, H, H2, I, I2, K; Basso et Tenore—Aa2, Bb, Bb2, Cc, Cc2, Dd, Dd2, Ee, Ee2, Ff, Ff2, Gg, Gg2, Hh, Hh2; Basso dell'organo—Aaa2, Bbb, Bbb2, Ccc, Ccc2, Ddd, Ddd2, Eee, Eee2, Fff, Fff2, Ggg.

2. Maria Caraci Vela, among others, has shown, particularly on mensural matters, that "le soluzioni iper-diplomatiche . . . che sono tuttora molto praticate dagli editori non danno alcun apporto chiarificatore—semmai offrono un ulteriore elemento di confusione, prestandosi ad interpretazioni scorrette o arbitrarie—e fanno della trascrizione un lavoro a metà" (hyper-diplomatic solutions, . . . still often adopted by editors, are no way clearer—they offer further elements of confusion, if anything, laying themselves open to erroneous or arbitrary interpretations—and leave the transcription as a half-done work). See her "Introduzione," in *La critica del testo musicale: Metodi e problemi della filologia musicale*, ed. Maria Caraci Vela (Lucca: Libreria musicale italiana, 1995), 31. A critical edition should *translate*, saving not necessarily the formal outline, but the 'spirit' of the text. In this perspective, the correct solution of

mensural problems—even if discussed in the critical notes—should in any case loom in the musical text itself. See Maria Caraci Vela, *La filologia musicale: Istituzioni, storia, strumenti critici,* vol. 1 (Lucca: Libreria musicale italiana, 2005), esp. 198.

3. See Roger Bowers, "Proportioned Notations in Banchieri's Theory and Monteverdi's Music," in *Performing Practice in Monteverdi's Music: The Historic-Philological Background—Proceedings of the International Congress, Goldsmiths' College, University of London (13–14 December 1993),* ed. Raffaello Monterosso, 63–64 (Cremona: Fondazione Claudio Monteverdi, 1995).

4. See Uwe Wolf, *Notation und Aufführungspraxis: Studien zur Wandel von Notenschrift und Notenbild in italienischen Musikdrucken der Jahre 1571–1630,* 2 vols. (Kassel: Meerseburger, 1992), esp. 1:89–93. See also, for instance, Rodobaldo Tibaldi's "Introduzione" to Oliviero Ballis, *Canzonette amorose spirituali a tre voci,* ed. Rodobaldo Tibaldi (Crema: Amici del Museo di Crema, 2001).